Gaining Insight Through

TACIT KNOWLEDGE

Achieving Full Understanding from Learning and Teaching

Ted Spickler

Printed by CreateSpace, an Amazon.com Company

Table of Contents

Acknowledgements

I am grateful to many friends who accepted my challenge to read various versions of the manuscript. Robert Schlemmer is a former teaching colleague of mine who was the first person to read the whole thing cover to cover and rather grimly warned me it was not fun and made suggestions. It takes a good friend to tell the truth. A similar friend, Bill Blakeslee, held my feet to the fire with many discussions about the topics in the book searching for inconsistencies and looking for errors. As a result of his concerns there are more changes in the book than I would like to acknowledge.

Some experienced teachers I know also read portions of the manuscript including Connie Bowers, Richard Drewyor, Ariana Erickson, and Kim Busey who offered a number of much needed suggestions regarding punctuation issues and questions of meaning.

Pat Jacobson set up a speaking engagement for me about tacit knowledge that was a strong reinforcement for me at a critical juncture. My son, Adrian Spickler, admitted that he was able to put into practice some useful suggestions in the book, another reinforcing moment.

I am especially indebted to a former teaching colleague, Dr. Virginia Shepard, who examined the entire document for instances of grammatical failures and pushed me to build better explanations of esoteric topics. I hope subsequent additions to the text remain in keeping with her expertise and helpful suggestions.

I appreciate very much the continual encouragement offered by Mrs. Donna Spickler who understood the lengthy periods of time I spent hidden away banging on computer keys while ignoring words she overheard that happily were not included in the manuscript!

Photo credits include:

Ariana Stathakis page 22
Jared Timper page 33
Clayton Fiest page 50
Autumn Fiest page 88

BIOGRAPHICAL NOTES:

In 1964 Ted become assistant professor of physics at West Liberty University in West Virginia. He became chairperson of the physics department, taught astronomy, intermediate physics, and took over the physical science course for students in the elementary teaching degree program. It was apparent these students were afraid of science and as the typical textbooks were clearly inappropriate, Ted discarded the book and created a new two-semester course sequence using inquiry-based, hands on science learning. The students responded well and as a result, Ted became interested in the problems of the psychology of learning.

He began a doctoral program in educational psychology at West Virginia University receiving that degree in 1983.

An unexpected opportunity sent his career off in a new direction-becoming manager of the new computerized "Laboratory Information Management System" at the New Martinsville Plant of Mobay Chemical Corporation. During his time in New Martinsville Ted volunteered with a Mobay chemist and a math professor from Bethany College to create an experimental hands-on, after-school science program for all fourteen elementary schools in Marshall County, West Virginia. The success of this effort depended in part on receiving a coordinated set of grants, one from the US Department of Education and the other from the National Science Foundation. Mobay (subsequently known as Bayer MaterialScience) took notice of the after-school science program and transferred Ted to Pittsburgh as one of their Science Education Coordinator's helping to guide the corporate science education outreach initiative called *Making Science Make Sense*. Bayer collaborated with the National Science Foundation and Ted became involved with NSF's "Local Systemic Change" initiative (introducing kit-based science teaching in school districts around the country). The partnership included associated programs sponsored by the National Sciences Resources Center of the National Academy of Science. Through these links Ted was able to help gain several NSF grants (totaling six million dollars) that triggered a local systemic change initiative in the five counties of the northern panhandle of West Virginia and another one in two counties around Charleston, South Carolina. His interest in problems of education continued at Bayer as a corporate trainer for Six Sigma, Continuous Improvement, ISO 9000, and Root Cause Analysis. Ted retired from Bayer in 2008.

Preface

In the early seventies, I was an assistant professor of physics at West Liberty State College in West Virginia and enjoyed investing residual time and energy exploring the philosophical foundations of science. Luckily, the philosophy professor there, Landon Kirchner, taught a special course in the philosophy of science; I was pleased to take a seat in his class. Kirchner's lectures on the contributions of **Michael Polanyi** to science and philosophy offered unanticipated revelations. I rushed to the library to find anything written about the mysterious Polanyi and his theory of tacit knowledge. To my surprise, there was nothing there except Polanyi's masterpiece, *Personal Knowledge*. I yanked it off the shelf (blowing away the accumulated dust) and devoured each delicious idea.

The limited number of references to Polanyi's work within educational psychology is one of many other surprises I later encountered. A description of his *theory of tacit knowledge* is hard to find despite its currency in the literature on corporate knowledge management, medical practice (especially nursing), and specialized niches in psychology and philosophy. I encourage the reader to examine Polanyi's own words directly (see the annotated bibliography). Be warned that he was a scholar and his thoughts are not easy to digest. I suspect some features of Polanyi's claims were sufficiently unpopular during the siege of behaviorism to overshadow his various powerful insights. Polanyi's interest in the nature of *inner conscious experience,* as revealed through his introspective observations, conflicted with Skinnerian behaviorism. In those days anyone thinking, talking, and writing about inner experience seemed out of touch with the scientific character of psychology. Now the cognitive revolution in psychology is throwing open a wide window allowing fresh examination of the *subconscious mental operations* described by Polanyi.

Curiously, you need to read this book in order to understand how to read it! I mean, understanding the process of comprehension is a prerequisite to making sense of the book. This problem is strangely circular and suggests you might consider reading the book twice.

Educationally related insights found in the tacit theory of knowledge are but a small part of the full theory of knowledge that Polanyi developed. What you find here is a tiny keyhole view that unfortunately overlooks most of his entire body of philosophical thought. Consult the bibliography for ideas on how to explore the full range of his views including his complete philosophy of science and the place of tacit knowing in art, culture, economics, as well as religion.

Comprehension through Insight

You are starting a popular review of tacit knowledge applied to understanding what it means to *comprehend* something initially difficult. I claim no contribution other than playing the role of detective, placing the theory of tacit knowledge into a current perspective showing how tacit knowing fits into the educational psychology of today. As you travel with me through these chapters, you are likely to notice that some revealed bits of advice about teaching and learning are not surprising and, in some cases, constitute common sense. However, I ask for your patience. Anticipate viewing the art and practice of gaining comprehension from a new perspective: a vantage point that organizes what you already know into a new and useful pattern. Watch how the structure of tacit knowledge brings clarity to *insight* and the functioning of unconscious processes. I will spiral gradually through the subject material looking to build an ever-deeper understanding of tacit knowledge. Just as a detective must search among the clues, I cycle back repeatedly, delving deeper with each revolution. The aim of the book is to plunge far enough into the mystery of comprehension and its companion, insight, to bring to the forefront some practical advice to the teacher/guide and to us as learners. The voyage takes us to the edge of what scientists know about how the mind works, and then we peer off into the distance beyond looking for relationships only dimly recognized by current science. The resulting view is refreshing and even makes sense within the context of neuroscience.

Our Purpose: To learn how to achieve comprehension by understanding how tacit knowledge is triggered and applied to teaching and learning.

Why should you care about this?

There are several reasons. The first is normal human curiosity. The underlying structure of mental comprehension and insight is potentially interesting and fun to know about. This book should appeal to a class of readers who are psychology junkies, "psycho-nerds" who read everything they can on how the mind works (I am among that group).

A more practical aim is that you may face the challenge of trying to understand something inherently difficult. Perhaps you are taking a class in school or college. I will offer help on how to guide your learning behaviors as you begin the struggle to comprehend difficult new concepts.

Perhaps you might be in the position of trying to teach a difficult idea to someone else or even a room full of students, (such as in a school setting). Tacit knowledge is largely missing from all the teaching pedagogies and theories offered in schools of education. This book could serve as adjunct reading in a college course on educational psychology or an offering in curriculum and instruction.

Lastly, information in this book might help a parent or member of the community judge alternative school instructional strategies during the regular waves of convulsive revisions society undergoes in a search for the best ways to teach the young.

Unfortunately, understanding the structure of learning as offered here does not come easily or quickly so detective work is necessary. A further note of warning: I am well aware that practicing teachers are fed up with theory. When you are trying to survive classrooms full of wriggling adolescents, the prospect of slogging through more theory is comparable to undergoing a root canal. I understand you might feel this journey is bogging down with too much theory; I hope you have the persistence to stick with it.

Visit my website at www.tacitknowledge.org to share various personal experiences in applications of tacit knowledge. As new information develops, I intend to add it to the website.

At the Beginning
The struggle to learn and understand difficult concepts

I claim that commercial education tends to ignore or gloss over teaching and learning techniques leading to the desirable outcome of full comprehension. As a result, I wrote this book mimicking a detective story searching among clues to seek clarification on how the mind achieves understanding. Sometimes comprehension occurs in a sudden burst, a special moment when everything comes together in a flash of comprehension. Psychologists identify this effect as the result of *insight*. At other times the understanding builds gradually, it sneaks up slowly so that you barely recognize a breakthrough has taken place. I am looking to uncover the **mental structure** explaining how this process of understanding works. By *structure,* I mean a scaffolding of mental activity that either leads to the "Aha!" moment or culminates in the gradual creation of a mental system of coherent thought that we recognize as *understanding*. Either way, you gain satisfaction from really knowing something that you did not know before.

Back in the olden days when I went to school, I was advised to listen carefully to the teacher, take good notes, read the textbook, and follow other timeworn techniques for learning. Despite that familiar advice, I found the process of learning varied widely from class to class and teacher to teacher. Not always understanding what I needed to do as an active learner, my achievement suffered as well as my psyche. I can now offer advice on learning and teaching based on Michael Polanyi's theory of tacit knowledge. I wish I could send this message backward in time to that younger "me" in those olden days of yesteryear.

Success at achieving comprehension is a consequence of applying *tacit knowledge*. Contemporary theories of education overlook this key element of mental performance and as a result, fail to explain how insight and comprehension develop inside the brain. I invite you to follow along with me as I explore these issues. If comprehension of difficult concepts is a central aim of learning, the uncovering of the hidden process that leads to such understanding should be of paramount importance to the problem of education. As we move forward through the book I will also briefly use tacit knowledge as a filter or lens through which a few fads and beliefs about education are judged with fresh eyes.

What do I mean by "mental structure" of comprehension?

Consider the common vacuum cleaner. It has a motor that mysteriously generates suction while connected to a tube aimed at dust bunnies and dirt. The suction pulls the dirt into a container.

I just described to you the *structure* of a vacuum cleaner. Now I attempt to do the same for an internal mental process called *tacit knowledge*. The word *structure* refers to a description of how something is built and how it works. We seek an explanation of the *theory of tacit knowledge* by first clarifying its structure. Notice that when referring to the vacuum cleaner, I glossed over critical details such as how the motor is designed and made. Similarly, I will choose to avoid details of the deeper aspects of the structure of tacit knowledge because at this time we lack adequate knowledge of neurological specifics. In other words, there seems to be some magic operating within the brain as well as in that vacuum cleaner.

Understanding comprehension

What takes place in the mind when we strive for comprehension and finally achieve it? An important piece of this desired explanation is found hidden within a scarce nugget of information almost completely forgotten today. Here is where our detective story begins. Imagine you are entering a gigantic bookstore like Barnes and Noble. Cast your eyes in all directions, looking up and down aisles bulging with books. See tables piled high with more books. Look among stacks of books jammed on shelves covering all available wall spaces. I claim the nugget we are looking for is not to be found anywhere in that entire building! Worse, if you were to examine every index at the end of all those thousands of books, you are very unlikely to find even the most cursory mention of this lost idea. A large university library will have one or two books of relevance buried deep in the stacks yet nearly impossible to find. Several journal articles are likely scattered here and there as well, but finding these few sources to uncover the hidden nugget is quite a challenge. The curious lack of information about this "secret" idea seems almost the result of a crazy conspiracy of silence, like some special knowledge only permitted among the cognoscenti of a closed philosophical society. I do not pretend such a fantastical claim is the case; the nugget is merely forgotten information, an item lost in the huge crush of knowledge generated throughout the past hundred years. Near his death, Polanyi was frustrated that his work might be dying with him. At least in the area of applicability to education I hope to remedy this neglect.

- **So what is this nugget?**
- **What does it mean?**

- **How does it help us clarify the structure of comprehension?**

Michael Polanyi's Tacit Theory of Knowledge

We begin by looking backward, starting around the middle of the twentieth century, to rediscover ideas developed by Michael Polanyi and found within his *theory of tacit knowledge* (Polanyi M. , Personal Knowledge, 1962).

First a note of clarification: when invoking tacit knowledge (such as found at the "Aha!" event) I do not mean making simple discoveries like finding where I lost my keys, or discovering my remote great grandfather in a census record. These actions may elicit a grateful feeling of accomplishment, but they pertain to a simple and less structured mental activity. Neither am I replicating what has become a popular publishing genre offering to help the reader on problem solving and lateral thinking. Instead, I am focused on understanding how we achieve that special exultant rush of comprehension - a mental breakthrough - that takes place when finally comprehending something really hard to understand (such as the central limit theorem in statistics or the conservation of angular momentum in physics or the structure of harmonies in a concerto for bassoon and orchestra). The task of climbing these difficult pillars of understanding is found in nearly all human endeavors from cooking to playing basketball. Insight sometimes occurs unexpectedly and apparently without conscious mental processing. You are unaware of the cognitive gears turning just before the insight flashes into your mind; it just shows up like magic. At other times, it grows slowly as if on little cat feet, builds consciously a little bit at a time until finally you realize you "got it"!

Can we take much of the mystery out of the magic?

I claim Polanyi did exactly that! Scientists lack interest in mysterious claims of semi-mystical activities lying at the heart of mental performance. For this reason, anecdotal descriptions of insight struggle against a bad reputation among research psychologists. As sophisticated tools of empirical investigation are developed and applied to the elusive character of insight, that reputation problem is easing and the field is now busy with effective experimentation. Increasingly we are getting away from the idea that insight lies beyond the capability of science to explain. Polanyi offered a theory that helps us look at insight from a useful perspective and serves as a launch pad into the science of the brain

Chapter One: Who Was Polanyi?

As detectives, we shall start at the beginning with the originating genius. Medical doctor, research chemist, economist, philosopher, and social scientist, Wikipedia defines him as a "polymath" which is a term currently replacing the phrase "Renaissance Man."

Born in Budapest (Austria-Hungary) in 1891, Michael Polanyi aimed for a medical degree at the University of Budapest. He was so attracted to pure science that he spent much of his studies there concentrating on physical chemistry specializing in adsorption on colloid surfaces. After graduating as a medical doctor, he was thrown into the Serbian front during World War I treating wounded soldiers. He found himself plopped unhappily into the middle of political and military turmoil at the beginning of his adult life. While at the front, Polanyi, not yet a card-carrying scientist, pursued a fascination with Nernst's heat theorem. This bold activity caught the attention of the iconic physicist, Albert Einstein, who engaged the young doctor in some interesting correspondence. Polanyi caught diphtheria and retreated to Budapest for recovery. While healing there he resumed his study of physical chemistry leading eventually to a doctorate on the adsorption of gasses.

Politics exerted a continuing influence on Polanyi's career. Just after the war, Austria-Hungary reconstituted itself as the Hungarian Democratic Republic and Polanyi, interested in promoting a new form of internationalism, accepted a position at the Ministry of Health. While there, he drafted plans for the demobilization of Hungary. Communists then took over the fledgling country, an event jolting Polanyi back into science. He took a position at the Kaiser Wilhelm Institute Fur Faserstoffchemie in Berlin (the MIT of its day). While there, he did pioneering work in chemical reaction theory using the new X-ray diffraction technique. He soon took over the chemical kinetics research group in Fritz Haber's Institute for Physical Chemistry and Electrochemistry and became professor at the University of Berlin. He led doctoral candidates in physical chemistry one of whom (Eugene Wigner) would later win the Nobel Prize. While at the Institute, he became an expert in X-Ray Crystallography and became head of the department of physical chemistry. In 1923, Polanyi married Magda Kemeny (a graduate student herself in chemical engineering) in a civil ceremony and began a family.

During his years in Germany, he produced over a hundred research publications and developed professional relationships with top scientists including Nobel Prize winners. Unfortunately, the unhappy force of politics and militarism intervened; Hitler came to power and Polanyi uprooted again. He wisely left Germany in 1933 for England where he continued his research in physical chemistry at the University of Manchester. Such was the power of Polanyi's scientific capability that a post doc serving under his tutelage (Melvin Calvin) also won the Nobel Prize. William Scott's comprehensive review of the scientific output of Michael Polanyi shows how his scientific and political experiences primed his mind to reflect upon the nature of doing science as well as provoking introspections into processes of thinking and creative activity (Scott, 1983).

The pull of other interests began to interfere with his focus on chemistry. His son, John Polanyi (another eventual Nobel Prize winner) characterized the father as a committed amateur (Polanyi J. C., 2005). While in Germany, Michael experienced the horror of hyperinflation as well as other social upheavals. His thoughts turned to economics and social systems. He had contacts in Soviet Russia and commenced a comparative study of free markets versus central planning. As World War II subsided, Polanyi, unsettled by the instability of social systems, immersed himself in the study of economics. This effort resulted in a book called *Full Employment and Free Trade*. Polanyi analyzed the flow of money in a society and deduced the need for some kind of limited influence from a central bank. He received considerable and favorable attention from professional economists for this contribution.

What led Polanyi to develop his theory of tacit knowledge?

Curiously, the effort began with the Russian revolution that initially attracted intellectuals to potential social improvements deriving from central government planning. Following the Marxist example of central planning in the new Russia, the role of a central authority in controlling the direction of scientific research became a topic of debate in England. As described in his slender volume, *Science, Faith and Society*, Polanyi traveled to the Soviet Union three times and held theoretical discussions with one of the key Marxist scholars, N. Bukahrin (eventually executed by Stalin). The discussions in Russia reinforced Polanyi's lack of enthusiasm for centralized planning when applied to managing scientific discovery. In order to counter the growing interest among British scientists for the centralized planning of scientific research, Polanyi realized he needed to argue from the strength of a **philosophy of science**. He feared the Marxist forces pervading intellectual thought aimed at a take-over of science for primarily political purposes. Threats to scientific freedom absorbed much of his attention over the remainder of his life.

The University of Manchester realized this preoccupation would flower under a different professorship and he took up residence in the department of economics and social studies. His introspective analysis into the philosophy of science and the characteristics of scientific discovery led to the development and explication of his theory of tacit knowledge. He showed how science was not the pure and objective pursuit of knowledge typically imagined but instead stood on a curiously squishy sounding, **internalized tacit component**. His new philosophy of science, a field with which he had no formal training, was not universally understood or appreciated by some scientists and philosophers although it seems to have had a noticeable effect on Thomas Kuhn (a famous philosopher of science). The so-called amateur continued during the last decades of his life to examine philosophical implications of tacit knowledge including its relation to art, religion, and social behavior. By 1945, Polanyi had successfully defended the need for independence and freedom in the pursuit of scientific discovery and subsequently the central planning movement for controlling scientific research died out.

Despite some thirty years of invited lectures at universities from all over the globe, Polanyi died in 1976 frustrated that his work appeared to have had limited impact. In a remarkable book, *Bunch of Amateurs*, Jack Hitt describes the special advantages held by those who are pigeon holed as mere amateurs. Hitt shows how a nonprofessional familiarity with a field of thought allows problems in that field to shine in a fresh way thus leading to unexpected discoveries (Hitt, 2012). Could the absence of references to tacit knowledge in the educational literature be attributable to an amateur status held by Michael Polanyi in that academic field?

Certainly when he published the first description of tacit knowledge, psychology had frozen into the force field of **behaviorism** where introspection about internal mental states was very much out of favor. Science was all about making observable measurements; hence, psychologists saw little of value coming from ideas pulled from a muddle of self-reflection. Scientists rarely esteem philosophical reflections on their field especially when implications of fuzzy "personal knowledge" stand between empirical observations and reality. Regardless of what anyone may think about the somewhat mystical setting of tacit knowledge, the discoveries of a scholar such as Michael Polanyi cry out for serious examination and necessarily constitute the foundation of this book.

I begin with an explanation of Polanyi's theory of tacit knowledge, and then extend it to the process of learning and teaching. After that, follow along as we detectives dig through current research looking for clarification about how tacit knowledge might operate inside the neuronal brain. Finally, we come back full circle to review how tacit knowledge guides us in learning and teaching.

I fear some of my rooting around in the technical details of contemporary research into psychology and neuroscience will prove too academic for some readers, but we really must investigate these new discoveries. Are Polanyi's revelations as true today as they were over 60 years ago?

Chapter Two: The Theory of Tacit Knowledge

Aha! Comprehension through Insight

Certainly, you are familiar with the experience of trying to understand something difficult. Despite diligent and lengthy study, your efforts eluded comprehension. After suffering through the seemingly endless frustrations of trying to learn an unfamiliar and complex idea, suddenly a mysterious, internal flash of understanding strikes. In a state of exultation, we cry out "Aha! Now I get it!" Despite the greatest care in expository brilliance, use of graphic aids, employment of hands on activities, reading assignments carefully designed to help us understand a new concept, our struggles operate as if an entrenched mental block is deliberately interfering with the ongoing effort to understand the issue.

I have a friend who operates out of his garage containing elaborate wood working tools. He makes artistic and highly precise items ranging from cutting boards to kitchen cabinets, all at a completely professional level of expertise (Busey, 2013). He was showing me one evening a computer program that offers a visual mechanism for designing projects. Images of carefully drawn parts rotate at his command within three-dimensional spaces and combine for examination and analysis. Tiny and quite mysterious icons surround the computer screen. I expressed amazement that learning to operate such a complicated program is possible. He admitted that several weeks of trial and error were required to gain some facility in using the program; all of a sudden, it came together in a flash and he "got it"! What did he get? The memorization of a particular set of linked key strokes. No, he "got" the whole thing, the overall structure of the program as if he climbed into the head of the programmer and could see how everything fit together. From that moment on, the various complex icons and key strokes began to make sense.

A similar struggle of my own comes to mind. I recall years of effort aimed at trying to learn physics; a subject infamous for being fearsomely difficult, fit only for either geniuses, insane persons, or those who likely enjoy periodic whippings. I was in neither of those categories and had to endure lengthy periods of high stress trying to understand pieces of this intricate and complex subject. One particular adventure in learning difficulty is seared into my emotional neurons to this day. I will show you a picture and its associated equation. The physics behind this horror story is not intended to gain your understanding, instead just follow my description of the torture I endured to finally grasp the meaning of the equation and how insight led to that breakthrough.

The piece of physics that confronted me is ubiquitous within the physical universe hence is found in all subfields of physics and engineering. Energy flows from one place to other places and a key mode of that transmission takes the form of a wave. To properly deal with all aspects of nature, physics seeks a precise language with which to describe the behaviors found in nature. The requisite language is that of mathematics.

On the next page is a picture of a wave. It could be a wave pulse on a string or an electric wave passing through space or the representation of pressure in a sound wave – makes no difference. The structure of this wave is mathematically described by the sine function known from trigonometry.

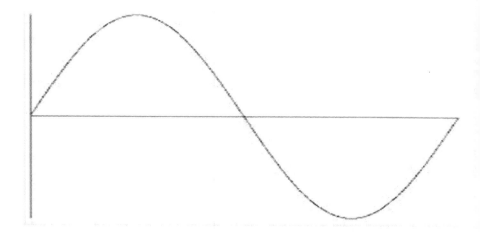

Here is the problem: imagine the wave moving from left to right with a certain speed (call that speed "**s**"). We are looking at a side view of the wave at some location "**x**" at a specific moment in time, "**t**." We want to know *how high* the wave is (on the vertical **y** axis) at a given moment of time. A formula tells us. I know, you hate formulas (publishers are famous for warning if a formula shows up in a book the author will crumble and die like a zombie). I take my chances – remember you need not understand this, just follow the description of my learning pains. The pain is the story here.

Y(x,t) = Asine*w*(t - x/s)

How does "(**t - x/s**)" tell us where we are on the sine curve at the moment of time "**t**", at location "**x**", when the wave is moving forward in the *positive* direction? There is a stupid minus sign stuck in that formula! My textbook failed to explain what the formula was saying, it just plopped the formula down on the page as if to say, there, eat it! Physics textbooks are known for their common phrase, "it is obvious that..." Whenever such a phrase pops up students know this means trouble because it can only be obvious to the professor. Anyway, I beat my head against all available walls trying to understand this crazy thing between the parentheses. I'll bet it took me several weeks of occasional staring and guessing and wishing, and self-recriminating about just being stupid when suddenly the understanding of that minus sign hit me like a box of physics books crashing down on my head. I just *KNEW* in a flash how that little piece of the equation worked! I did not consciously figure it out, the idea splashed into my mind fully formed and at that microsecond I also knew something else, my understanding was certainly *correct*.

Entire books exist describing these moments. One of the earliest publications collected stories told by mathematicians and scientists about their insightful experiences (Hadamard, 1973). Another examined the role of the unconscious in developing creative ideas. Many examples came from Hadamards own experience and those of others who he personally knew (Jones, 2012).

Why does this painful process take so long? Why is the breakthrough often preceded by lengthy and apparently unconscious mental gymnastics? What is happening inside our mind that requires this excruciating interval of time before the final moment of exultant breakthrough? How can understanding this "Aha!" effect offer enlightenment to the structuring of mental behavior needed for guiding our own learning? Surely educational psychologists have settled these questions by now, but a perusal of the literature leaves one strangely disquieted.

In his book, *The Eureka Effect*, David Perkins sets out to find a psychological explanation for what he calls the "cognitive snap" (we recognize this as the "Aha!" moment). After surveying a number of psychological explanations and finding them inadequate, he concludes that the snap is really just ordinary garden variety "comprehension." Suddenly the mind understands something in a flash of comprehension. In a most telling paragraph, he admits that comprehension is not itself well understood. He considers the process to be quite a mystery as psychologists, philosophers, and other research scientists studying brain functioning still puzzle over how the mind does it (Perkins, 2000).

Topolinski and Reber review the considerable amount of research conducted and published on brain processes underlying the basis of insight but admit that so far no real explanation of the experience of insight has come forth (Topolinski & Reber, 2010). Other current researchers into the nature of insight express similar opinions. They have hypotheses; experimental tests are run to check the hypotheses, but no comprehensive structure of explanation pops out and there is disagreement among these experts.

Levels of explanation

Technical explanations for just about anything vary in complexity depending upon the depth of the dive into the subject. Neuroscientists examine nerve fibers so their explanations of behavior takes place at a microscopic level dealing with thousands of connections (called synapses) between neurons. Cognitive psychologists conduct amazing and elaborate experiments measuring behavior to infer internal mental mechanisms at work (not observable under a microscope). On the other hand, philosophers choose to debate ideas at abstract levels embedded within clouds of impenetrable terminology. Isaac Newton explained gravity by invoking a precisely defined (yet still magic) force between masses, and then Einstein came along and carved out fluctuations in space-time to explain the same thing. I learned how to drive a car without needing to calculate the forces between gears in the transmission, yet it helps if the driver realizes that an engine is beneath the hood needing gasoline, and starts from a burst of electricity surging out of the battery. These are all examples of differing levels of explanation.

We will now examine the nature of insight and comprehension, not initially at the explanatory level of firing synapses, but instead at a level relying upon Polanyi's representation for awareness and thought. His ideas about the components of mental structure help us make sense of insight in a practical manner. Getting there, however, will take some effort on your part. Later we will examine other, deeper levels of explanation, to gain a greater understanding of the theory of tacit knowledge.

Comprehension

Do you remember being in school semi-listening to a teacher droning on while your thoughts danced far away, perhaps out the window, to distant places and to other times? Because of these moments, we became accustomed to regarding school learning as a passive activity. Some famous person, not ourselves, accomplished a magical, creative breakthrough leaving to us the onerous task of mastering that seemingly long dead knowledge. Formal conventional schooling aims at jamming facts into our brains through the interventions of a teacher and textbook. Teachers are expected to stuff knowledge into minds as if through intravenous brain feeding. Such an admittedly outdated process of education is adequate if we are satisfied with memorizing facts for a test. I will argue here that we need to seek a deeper level of learning - full comprehension. New theories and educational practices do aim at developing comprehension yet appear within tangles of technical disagreement. The theory of tacit knowledge offers to us an explanation for a desired form of deeper understanding. As detectives we must search for clues and the most critical clue is about to be unearthed.

I need to warn you that Polanyi uses the word "**particulars**" in a special way. Any complex idea (like how a formula works) is made of many little bits of facts and possibly even relationships between some of the facts. Teachers may try, but do not actually stuff these bits and facts into a blank mind. The "particulars" do need to get in there of course, but once inside the brain, the learner must actively create, inside their private brain-space, the *integration* of all these needed *individual particulars* together into a full *comprehension.* **The process Polanyi called "integration" is a mental act combining particulars together in a certain way that builds an understanding of "the whole thing."** Your understanding of what I just wrote is a key aim for this book. Do not expect to understand what I just said all at once, learning does not usually work that way. I will return and recycle through this idea several times. Be patient.

We will use Polanyi's tacit theory of knowledge to understand the structure of the "Aha!" moment and its resulting *comprehension.* I can then offer answers to your concerns about how to learn something difficult as well as how to help someone else accomplish that same end. Finally we now get to dig into the theory that Polanyi developed in the mid-fifties of the last century.

What is the Theory of Tacit Knowledge?

The dictionary instructs us that "tacit" refers to a thought or idea that is understood without being expressed. Polanyi claims that tacit knowledge cannot be directly communicated even if you try hard to do so. You cannot explicitly communicate the essence of the understandings hidden in the form of tacit knowledge because this is a kind of experiential knowledge not readily spelled out in symbolic form. The best way to gain a handle on this idea is by thinking through some practical examples. We begin with physical skills but ultimately aim at understanding mental representations.

Recall the difficulty you had learning to ride a bicycle. At first, the task of keeping the wobbly machine upright seemed nearly impossible and demanded intense concentration. Every muscular exertion took conscious awareness and mental control. Your performance was clumsy and often resulted in falling upon the ground; a considerable contrast to the skillful rider you eventually became. Now imagine that years later you are trying to teach this same skill to a new hesitant rider. A verbal description of how to handle the bicycle is not adequate and you will find that you cannot put words to those actions needed to keep the bicycle upright. You can offer hints and guidance but there is a "tacit knowledge" structured within your mind-body system that knows how to ride a bicycle. You cannot express that knowledge in a symbolic fashion readily available to the learner. In other words, the neophyte rider cannot find the answer written in a book (although carefully crafted explicit information does carry some value).

The tacit form of knowledge is not limited to physical skills. A chess champion knows more about playing chess than can be put into a sequence of words. A great composer writes a symphonic masterpiece but has trouble *explicitly* passing that skill on to someone else. The mathematician constructs insightful proofs but can only show others the systematic process through the advantage of hindsight. Polanyi explained this apparent human deficiency by describing a mental structure he called **subsidiary awareness** needed to perform skillful acts. This idea of a subsidiary awareness is not easy to grasp and will occupy our attention throughout the book. Many clues are needed to bring this subtle idea into a state of comprehension. One of the problems I have explaining Polanyi comes from a need to use specific terminology he invented. As with mathematics, this characteristic serves as a barrier to your eventual understanding.

The Structure of Awareness

Polanyi identified two different kinds of human awareness. The obvious one is your explicit attention to some sensation or perceptual detail. He called this **focal awareness.** It occurs when you consciously focus upon the "thing" your awareness is aiming at. When searching on the ground for a lost set of keys, your consciousness is directed as if a laser beam is scanning the ground looking intently at everything seen until the keys come into view. We focus our eyes, ears, or pressure sensations from the skin when directing focal attention to whatever is causing that sensory input. You can also focus attention on an internal thought in the same manner.

The second kind of awareness is difficult to communicate and understand. Polanyi called it **subsidiary** awareness and it is indeed rather mysterious. The best way to begin grasping at what he meant is by looking at additional examples. Let us begin with a common skill known as *reading*. As you read these words, you are conscious of the meaning *behind* the words and recognize the act of reading as an effort of consciousness. However, are you looking closely at the shape of each letter in the word? Must you consciously identify each letter one by one and then from this collection of letters figure out the complete word? Do you then carefully put all the words together in a sentence and solve the puzzle of their meaning? No, instead you are typically aware of the meaning of an entire phrase as a single thought. You have a *subsidiary awareness* of the letters, their shapes, and the combination of the letters into words. You *tacitly construct* the full meaning of the sentence from these individual words so that your *focal* awareness is aimed at the **meaning** of the entire sentence. The meaning of the sentence is the target of your focal awareness. A curious example of this effect recently spread throughout the internet (Rawlinson, 1976):

Olny srmat poelpe can raed tihs.
I cdnuolt blveiee taht I cluod aulaclty uesdnatnrd waht I was rdanieg. The phaonmneal pweor of the hmuan mnid, aoccdrnig to a rscheearch at Cmabrigde Uinervtisy, it deosn't mttaer in waht oredr the ltteers in a wrod are, the olny iprmoatnt tihng is taht the frist and lsat ltteer be in the rghit pclae. The rset can be a taotl mses and you can sitll raed it wouthit a porbelm. Tihs is bcuseae the huamn mnid deos not raed ervey lteter by istlef, but the wrod as a wlohe. Amzanig huh?

Yes, this is amazing because we take subsidiary awareness so much for granted. The word *subsidiary* refers to a varying degree of unconsciousness of the awareness. Subsidiary means, "subordinate too"; in this case subsidiary awareness is subordinate to focal awareness. The subsidiary awareness may range from full unconsciousness upwards to a weak form of consciousness. To gain further understanding of what Polanyi meant we will later follow some clues found in contemporary research into cognitive psychology and neuroscience. Meanwhile try to settle upon the meaning of "subsidiary" as demonstrated by this next example.

The process of reading is similar to the process of successfully riding a bicycle. You do not direct conscious awareness to each muscular movement in order to keep the bicycle upright just as you do not consciously figure out each letter when constructing words while reading. If you directed your focal attention to each muscular action of your body while bike riding, you would soon find yourself staring at the sky with skinned knees. Likewise, if you direct focal attention, while reading, to the precise shape and identity of each letter in every word, you slow down and gradually lose track of the meaning of the words. In order to gain meaning from written words, you must use the skill (acquired from years of practice) that allows you to attend to the form of the words in a subsidiary manner. We have a **subsidiary awareness** of the shapes of letters and their coherence into words so that we may focally attend to the full meaning of the many words all taken at once. When you break your subsidiary awareness of the many letters and words by looking closely at the shape of each letter, you break the connection between subsidiary and focal knowledge and then you lose awareness of the end target, which is the meaning behind the writing.

Wow, did you follow all that? Sentences like those just above make reading difficult and require focused attention.

Examples of this effect are found everywhere. When first learning to play a musical instrument, such as a recorder (it looks like a simple clarinet that behaves more like a flute), you must direct focal attention to making your fingers behave. For a particular desired note to sound, selected holes carefully drilled into the recorder are covered up while others are left open. With conscious effort, you decode the little black dots on a page of music into finger arrangements. Blow into the recorder and if the fingers are set correctly, you get the right note. That finger placement  took a long time to figure out and then the next note is carefully constructed. What comes of this effort is hardly called music. Practice over many years automates the skill allowing for a gradual shifting of your focal attention **away** from intricate fingerings **to** the overall musical outcome. *You rely on subsidiary awareness of all individual particular muscular movements in order to enjoy focal awareness of the shape and flow of the music.*

I bet you can find additional examples of what I am talking about from your own experience. Any special skill you have will illustrate the two types of awareness as well as the **integration** of all the needed bits of knowledge to accomplish your skillful act. This pattern shows up in the tacit knowledge of cooks who can taste in their imagination the consequence of adding a teaspoon of this or a dash of that into a stew. I marvel at the communication between my wife and her daughter when they discuss a recipe. One of them suggests adding a pinch of such and such, the other responds to an imagining of the resulting taste.

The list of potential skills is endless but should not be considered limited to just a physical skill attained from years of manual practice. The resulting tacit knowledge is found in mental feats of accomplishment such as exhibited by a physicist building theories of the universe or a programmer grasping the structure of a computer software package.

Are you still unsure about this tacit stuff?

It's not surprising because your understanding of tacit knowledge must come from inside you and not from anyone or Polanyi, or this book. There are subsidiary particulars embedded within any tacit understanding including the understanding of tacit knowledge itself! In order to understand something complex the necessary subsidiary particulars must be **in** your head and then united by a *tacit integration*. That process does not occur until your mind is ready to leap across a logical gap in the brain (sometimes triggering the "Aha!" feeling). *Tacit integration* is another clue in the search for the theory of tacit knowledge. These clues will be re-examined again as we move forward toward building a full, comprehensive picture explaining how we comprehend difficult ideas.

You may sometimes need to take a break and come back later to read a section like this over again. You may need to take a break then come back for more focal concentration. Once you see how to map these ideas into your own experience, you will better understand the meaning of tacit knowledge. If you are still uncertain about what all this means, just keep plowing ahead. Curiously, we mysteriously "know" when we understand something and similarly we know when we do not. If you stop right here with your hands thrown up in confusion and despair, just bear in mind that the detective journey is not finished.

Polanyi introduced additional terms that help clarify the structure of his thinking; a description of a few of them will now help establish further the meaning of tacit knowledge.

Subsidiary Particulars

Polanyi uses that mysterious phrase "subsidiary particulars" to include all the sub-elements to which you must subconsciously attend in order to be aware of something larger to which the elements point. Do not let that last sentence throw you, review it again and make sense out of it. Those icons and special key strokes in a drawing program are all subsidiary particulars. Subsidiary in that you are not explicitly (focally) conscious of each command, yet you do use an "off to the side" awareness of these particulars to form a focal awareness of the whole thing (such as how the software package is structured). As previously described, the specific fingerings when playing a musical instrument also constitute subsidiary particulars as well as the many muscular movements needed to keep a bicycle upright and moving forward, as well as the specific technical details of a scientific theory. Unfortunately, the phrase "subsidiary particulars" is clumsy and awkward but it points to a crucial element within Polanyi's tacit theory of knowledge and as such, we will need to stick with the phrase to maintain continuity with other references and writings about tacit knowledge.

Subsidiary particulars are not only found within the realm of physical expertise. Abstract mental complexities (such as trigonometry) include subsidiary particulars that exist within the mind and are used to construct an integrated focal understanding of the mathematical whole to which they contribute.

From-To

A special relationship is found between the subsidiary particulars and the focal target to which they contribute. Polanyi refers to a *"from-to"* effect. Your mind focally attends *to the whole* (that which you desire to understand) by tacitly integrating *from* the subsidiary particulars. This effect sometimes finalizes when the "Aha!" occurs. If you direct your focal conscious attention to one of the many subsidiary particulars, you break the "from-to" relationship and the specific particular no longer serves its subsidiary role to aim attention to the whole. For example, you can mess with the mind of a golfer by asking for a description of how they grasp their club. That request throws the golfers focal attention to a subsidiary particular and ruins the stroke! When the subsidiary particular is being used tacitly, it becomes, in a sense, transparent, and we use our tacit awareness of it to look past it and beyond it to the broader whole to which it contributes, (the golf swing becomes automatic and effective).

Working backwards from the whole to various particulars is a process that gives meaning to the particular. If you to covered up most of the image of a face except for the area immediately around the eyes, you will be hard pressed to recognize an emotion projected by the subtle features of the eyes alone. The meaning of the subsidiary particulars (in this case specific eye characteristics) is lost because we do not have access to the other particulars of the face allowing us to recognize, through a tacit integration, the whole being of the person we are examining. When looked at focally, at close range, without benefit of the other particulars, a specific particular loses its meaning.

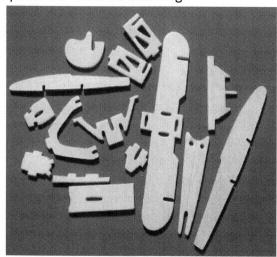

Here is a visual analogy. Look at this photograph containing a number of pieces and parts for making something. While looking at these parts you might "see" what they are supposed to construct. Analogously, if you were searching for the comprehension of an idea, all the parts need to be there and need to fit together in the mind. The pieces are likely to be only a confusing jumble of crazy shapes. Each item by itself carries little to no meaning. When placed together as a whole, they all fit into a pattern that gives each part its meaning. To make the analogy more real I have added a few parts that do not belong (representing misconceptions and errors). The presence of things that do not belong makes it harder for the mind to form the tacit integration creating the "whole" to which all the parts contribute. As a further nod to reality, I have left out some parts representing typically missing information. Without all the parts, the mind has a hard task forming the tacit integration.

When confronted with pieces and parts, you typically use explicit powers of conscious reasoning to construct a guess as to what these parts might have in common. **Immersion** in sources of additional information and feedback from an attentive teacher may serve to eliminate from your mind some errors and add the other individual particulars needed to figure out what these parts mean. This example is just an analogy. I am trying to illustrate **subconscious processing** of abstract ideas rather than the use of explicit conscious reasoning. Now look at a more complete set of parts with the misconceptions removed.

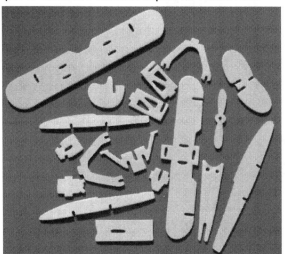

You might notice a thing that looks like a propeller and several shapes that remind you of wings. Perhaps this set of parts join together to create a "whole" that we may associate with the name *airplane.* There are however still lots of weird shapes that carry no explicit meaning. Generating an "Aha!" moment may need the operation of additional immersion time (looking carefully at the parts) and some **incubation** (taking a break and doing something else). I do not expect that to happen here; instead, I will offer you an image on a following page that shows how all the subsidiary particulars do fit together hence pointing to the whole thing. Bear in mind that conscious reasoning is a route to understanding. I do not intend to rule out that mode of comprehension; we are concerned here primarily with the development of tacit knowledge since that process is not so well recognized or understood.

Indwelling

Many examples are needed, many clues, to bring the tacit theory into full perspective. Here is another one. What do you mean when you say you *know* a person? When you say you know someone, you mean more than the simple statement that you are aware the person exists or that you have met that person at one time or another. You know a person when you have a sense of the personality and belief states behind the behavior of that person. You can thus predict behavior given some circumstance. Polanyi would say that we **dwell-in** the various subsidiary particulars that make up the person. You tacitly absorb the facial expression of the person and as a result seem to feel something of what that person is feeling. It is insufficient to be focally (deliberately) conscious of the persons features. A systematic, logical analysis of the person from these features is clumsy and slow. The tacit indwelling process on the other hand takes in lots of detail and all at once leaving no time for conscious analysis. I just described a function that lies at the heart of what we sometimes call **intuition**. Indwelling means to absorb into yourself (into your mind/body system), the many sense elements that direct you to be focally aware of what those elements collectively describe. How do you know a person is sad? The sense of sadness remains in your focal awareness because you indwell in all the subtle features pointing to sadness. The focal center of your consciousness is the awareness of the sadness. To know this sadness you must be aware, in a subsidiary manner, of all the subtle features and behaviors (the subsidiary particulars) of the person in a way that, while not directly conscious, leads you to be conscious of the feeling inside. This act illustrates the structure of tacit knowledge. We indwell (inhabit) in all those subtle features and, as a result, become focally aware of a person before us who seems to be sad.

Michael Polanyi named his book that outlined all these ideas *Personal Knowledge*. The indwelling feature just described gives rise to that sense our knowledge is personal more than explicit.

Switch gears for a moment. Look at the "whole" that a subsidiary awareness of the previously photographed parts constructs. The photo shows that it is indeed an airplane.

There is a potential confusion about tacit knowledge. My reference to the insight moment when all the subsidiary particulars suddenly cohere suggests that an Aha event is a necessary result of tacit integrations. The structure of tacit knowing does not always require sudden integrations. Physical skill development takes time and the fine-tuning of skill can spread out over a long period. You still need reliance on the subsidiary particulars to attend to the whole to which they all contribute. Sometimes the integration occurs suddenly hence, the Aha moment, but such an event is not required to generate knowledge from a tacit standpoint. The structure of tacit knowledge goes beyond explaining just the insight event. Comprehension can sneak up on you gradually.

The detective needs yet another set of clues with a different kind of example. I conducted an experiment testing the effect of indwelling using college students in a college physical science class. This was not an exercise in reading the characteristics of a person but instead was all about embedding students into a physical system. Usually laboratory exercises ask learners to make measurements on a physical parameter (such as pressure) by using an instrument that has a scale and requires reading numbers off the scale. What do you do with the numbers? Punch them into a formula and turn the crank – out comes another number. But what does the result really mean?

Indwelling vs barriers

When learning science and engineering, measurements are typically embedded within a laboratory exercise designed to judge the utility of a hypothesis. These measurement actions can curiously place a barrier between the student and the phenomena in question. The barrier occurs because a measurement of the physical phenomena interferes with a direct bodily sensation of it. A voltmeter measures one aspect of electricity existing between two electrodes by offering up a number seen on the face of the meter but experiencing an electric shock confronts the body with direct interaction with the electricity. To explore this barrier effect further, I added interventions to usual laboratory exercises by having students embed their bodily sensations into the activity in addition to making the usual measurements. For example, the notion of pressure is calculated by measuring the weight of an

object divided by another measurement of the contact area. The result is a number expressing the force per unit area. Subsidiary particulars include the idea of a force and the meaning of area (which includes length multiplied by width). The idea of pressure exists in an abstract realm unless the area and force are consciously felt. To accomplish a feeling experience, I cut a simple block of wood and hammered into it a wide headed nail partway into the wood on one side. Now a student can directly sense what the wood block weighs while it sits on their hand and then, by

flipping the block over, and balancing it carefully, the same weight is distributed over a smaller area (nail head) hence offering a feeling of greater pressure. The numerical value of pressure is easily calculated but the number is an abstraction. The *feeling* on the palm of the hand is a direct experience. The mind/body system can indwell within that feeling.

Other phenomena experienced by students may include density, which, as a concept, remains abstract unless lengths, widths and heights are measured, multiplied into volumes, and then divided by measurements of weight. Learners need exposure to a variety of differently sized blocks including exercises in guessing volume and weight, all in addition to performing calculations that lead to numerical values of density. The bodily sensation of density comes from comparing differently sized blocks made from different materials. Calculations should accompany direct experience if indwelling is to occur.

Electric currents behave as a mysterious, unseen flow of something initially incomprehensible. Since electricity is not directly observable, indwelling of the invisible is aided through use of an analogy. Create series and parallel "circuits" using water flowing through plastic tubes. This constructed device offers learners a direct visible experience of something like current flowing in wires. They can compare observations of water flowing through tubes to real electricity flowing through wires.

I tested Polanyi's theories by exposing an experimental group of students to a number of these exercises where, instead of just making measurements, they **directly felt the phenomena**. A separate control group of students only made the measurements. Summative tests revealed significant differences in comprehension between these two groups of students. The experimental results suggest that indwelling exercises help students develop a more complete sense of understanding for the felt physical effects as opposed to what happens when only performing explicit, abstract measurements followed by calculations. The felt things are subsidiary particulars and indwelling in those particulars helps to generate tacit integrations (comprehension). For example, comprehension of pressure as the "whole" requires reliance on weight and area as subsidiary particulars (Spickler, 1983).

Tacit Integration (the insight moment)

Three parts are required to complete the operation of tacit knowledge. First are the many particulars making up the "whole" and their need to be experienced in a special *subsidiary* manner. Second is the focal target to which these particulars point. Third is the person who does the indwelling and who produces the integration of all the particulars into recognition of that focal target. If you do not have the *active involvement* of a **person at the center**, there is no tacit knowledge formed (can a computer form tacit knowledge?). The process of integrating all the subsidiary particulars into a focal awareness is a personal act of the mind. A skillful and creative act is rarely acquired from only reading a book, listening to a lecture, or programming instructions into a computer. The mental movement toward integration usually takes place over time, involves the exercise of focused mental exertion, and is a creative act. Once the integration takes place, we say comprehension is achieved. If it happens suddenly, the term for this result is *insight* and psychologists are increasingly adept at designing experiments to tease out its secrets.

Barriers exist that interfere with the creation of tacit integrations. Learning for comprehension is the result of an initial conscious effort. The juggling of particulars (that need to become subsidiary) begins with the operation of focused consciousness. At first we direct focal attention to the particulars, gather them up, and hope eventually for them to become subsidiary in nature. That transformation is not willed into existence by our desiring minds. The path to getting to that moment when all the particulars are united through their subsidiary transparency is just ordinary hard work. How can we help the mind do all of this subterranean manipulation? Let us look at the **barriers** carefully but first check a comparison between tacit knowledge and its opposite.

Not tacit

Is there a form of knowledge that is not tacit? The American Heritage Dictionary describes *knowledge* as the broadest noun referencing that, which is "known." Knowledge includes facts, ideas, understandings, and the totality of that which is known. A simple fact is usually easy to communicate in a symbolic form to someone else. We may determine the current room temperature by reading a thermometer and then pass along that temperature reading in the form of a written or verbal statement such as:

The temperature is 72 degrees.

Recognition of this simple fact does not require tacit knowledge (unless you dig into the process by which the thermometer measures temperature). I will not become embroiled here in the scientific analysis of temperature measurement when asking the simple question, "how hot is it?" We are content with a direct numerical answer. Such simple factual answers that are communicated by symbolic means do not constitute tacit knowledge **except** when employing reliance on a bodily capacity to recognize and sense "hotness" or "coldness" of the reported number. Many persons do not have a tacit sense of hotness or coldness when the temperature is reported in degrees centigrade. If I were to tell you the temperature is 22 degrees Centigrade, some readers will have no feeling sense of how that corresponds to hotness or coldness. The measurement is just a number hence is explicit, not tacit, but the *indwelled sense* of what that number *means* in a recognized measurement system has a tacit component. There are two separate communications going on with temperature. In one case, the measured temperature is an explicit number hence not tacit knowledge but at the same time, we have a tacit sense of what the number means in a bodily sense as long as we have a tacit comprehension of the measurement scale. Another example is the "knowing" of distance. The measurement of a distance, say, how far is it to drive to work, makes sense to us when given in miles (an explicit number) but if expressed in kilometers we may have only a numerical value without the tacit sense of what that number means. Folks in Europe have an opposite experience since they use the metric system.

If you can provide written instructions for accomplishing an act, the performance of that act does not require tacit knowledge. Although using the Microsoft windows computer resulted in my learning how to do many things, a few arcane acts of computer shenanigans are not yet embedded reliably in my brain so I wrote "cheat sheets" that I follow to accomplish these more complex procedures. The act of doing this is not an example of tacit knowledge.

When reporting on the colors of the rainbow I can confidently spout off the words: Violet, Indigo, Blue, Green, Yellow, Orange, and Red. I have memorized an acronym that allows me to do that. The acronym is "VIBGYOR"; this is not tacit knowledge. There are skeptics who carry the counter examples to an extreme claiming that all knowledge is explicit. They insist that so called tacit is just some mystical leftover from old philosophical ramblings no longer relevant in the modern world of science (Loughlin, 2010). We will look at these negative opinions later as they offer further clues on our detective journey. Polanyi claimed the opposite. All explicit knowledge has, at its heart, a foundation in tacit knowledge.

The Logical Gap

Forming a tacit integration of the subsidiary particulars swirling around a new concept that we are trying to understand is difficult. Schooling is a formal approach society arranges for each of us to develop skills and knowledge about a wide body of topics deemed important for us to know and understand. Teachers and textbooks surround us in an effort to push the development of this knowledge but many students find the process difficult, stressful, and of little obvious benefit hence resort to a simple memorization of facts (called cramming the night before a test). The logical, formal, approach to learning something complex requires explicating systematically, all the details of that complicated "thing" in a careful, controlled, and rational manner. This action is accomplished with the printed word, aided by the verbal display of a hopefully inspired teacher, incorporation of help from struggling peers, and by direct immersion in the difficult thing (experience). Sometimes, as students, we remain puzzled after being led by the hand through these various explanations and experiences. As a consequence we end up concluding that we are either too dim witted to understand the mess or are being exposed to an inadequate explanation. The reality of the learning process is thus misperceived. After listening to the teacher without comprehension, reading passages in the text and other offered books to no avail, then asking a friend for help, the frustration over a failure to understand grows to a breaking point. Drop the problem and escape. Come back at another time somewhat refreshed but still, perhaps, to additional failure. No understanding has yet arrived (remember my formula example). After an unpredictable amount of time and concentrated effort punctuated by relief pursuing other tasks, the desired moment may suddenly hit in a flash. For some persons they may wake up in the middle of the night triumphant with sudden understanding. Others are surprised as if jolted by a bolt from the blue while mowing the lawn or engaged in some otherwise unrelated activity. The moment of insight triggers feelings of elation, excitement, and relief but can curiously elicit anger. For example, why did the understanding of this take so long – or why didn't someone just explain it to me correctly the first time? Some observers have called the event "transformational," others note that what they suddenly "see" cannot be described by words. All the details suddenly fall into place with linkages connecting various pieces and parts into a complete and satisfying mental tapestry. Teachers report on the delight they take in seeing this moment strike their students; an effect that, in many cases, provides a teacher with the greatest reward in their profession. We sometimes wonder why someone did not just explain the concept to us in the beginning, in the right way. In fact there is no best way to configure an explanation since understanding comes not from the explanation itself but from within our own *creativity*. The mind must integrate all by itself the various subsidiary particulars making up the concept. The teacher cannot do this for us, our friend cannot do this for us, the book does not do it, we do it ourselves; it is an act of creativity working deep within our own minds.

A *logical gap* exists prior to forming this tacit integration and the creative imagination is required to leap over the gap. It is at the "gap crossing moment" that we may feel a sudden rush of understanding and exultantly cry out, "Aha!" The insight experience is the moment of true learning where individual particulars leading to the understanding are suddenly perceived in the subsidiary sense rather than being focally examined individually. When the mind consciously dwells upon individual parts of the whole, we can only perceive these parts separately, by themselves, and therefore cannot recognize the whole to which they contribute. Only after the creative and personal act of integration, can we perceive all these parts in the new, tacit way thus opening up that personal discovery of understanding. The teacher can bring the student up to the gap and offer a number of information bits, pointing the way across, but the student does the leap and upon reaching the other side suddenly experiences the "Aha!" which comes from finally achieving full comprehension. Thus we have Polanyi's famous statement that "we know more than we can tell" (Polanyi M. , The Tacit Dimension, 1967) meaning that *nobody can explicitly tell you enough to bring about the gap crossing event*. The tacit integration is your own creative act and once acquired you find that your comprehension now includes knowing more than you can tell someone else.

Teachers are familiar with the exultant pleasure on display when a student experiences the moment of integration. In a newspaper article, Paige Coker, who teaches sixth to eighth grade students in the gifted program at Ware County Middle School, described her pleasure in teaching because of the help she offered to the students to reach that desired event of understanding:

'...to see that 'ah ha!' moment of recognition. Their eyes light up and you can see the excitement and understanding when they get the concept. That is what it's all about for me' (Stepzinski, 2006).

You do not consciously control this creative act of tacit integration. Sometimes time is required for the individual particulars to simmer in the background of the mind until finally that wonderful moment occurs when everything coalesces and you suddenly understand. No matter how many times the teacher goes over and over the explanation, no matter how many friends try to help you, no matter how many different portions of books you desperately read, you will not understand, you cannot understand, until the deep creativity of your own imagination places all of the stuff together into a tacit whole. This integration process does not mean you can kick back, relax and reject help. Do not skip over examining the explanations in various texts doing nothing until inspiration hits. All of the cognitive activity occurring through study and hard conscious thinking is necessary to feed the brain with raw material. Just realize that it is not the books, or the teacher, or the friends, who put understanding into your head. **It is your own mind doing the most critical part of the task of learning, the task of forming the tacit integration of all those individual pieces contributing to the whole.**

We do not sufficiently honor the learner as part of the commercial process of education. Memorizing is a tedious and passive behavior but true learning, forming tacit integrations of many individual particulars, is an act of personal creativity. The learners are creating the knowledge for themselves. In this sense when you form a tacit integration for the first time and experience that exultant "Aha!" you make the material your own. You own that knowledge; it belongs to you and not just to the book, or to the teacher, or only to the white haired old famous discoverer of whatever it is that you just understood. Certainly these other persons and sources of knowledge own the material in their own way but nobody can slight your ownership of the concept now integrated by you in that special tacit way.

Let us follow the self-reported behavior of some famous thinkers and see if you can recognize tacit processes at work. Perhaps the brilliant mathematician and physicist Henri Poincare described the most published example of a self-reported "Aha!" moment. He became fascinated with how his mind worked when discovering a new principle of mathematics. A book called *The Foundations of Science* (The Science Press, 1913) translated his self-reports into English and in chapter three, *Mathematical Creation*, we find a detailed description of an insight process regarding *Fuchsian Functions* (about which we are pleased to know nothing whatever). Poincare said:

"For fifteen days I strove to prove that there could not be any functions like those I have since called Fuchsian. I was then very ignorant; every day I seated myself at my worktable, stayed an hour or two, tried a great number of combinations and reached no results. One evening, contrary to my custom, I drank black coffee and could not sleep. Ideas rose in crowds; I felt them collide until pairs interlocked, so to speak, making a stable combination. By the next morning I had established the existence of a class of Fuchsian functions, those which come from the hypergeometric series. I had only to write out the results, which took but a few hours....Just at this time I left Caen, where I was then living, to go on a geologic excursion [*Poincare, among other accomplishments, was a trained mining engineer*] under the auspices of the school of mines. The changes of travel made me forget my mathematical work. Having reached Coutances, we entered an omnibus to go someplace or other. At the moment when I put my foot on the step, the idea came to me, without anything in my former thoughts seeming to have paved the way for it, that the transformations I had used to define Fuchsian functions were identical with those in non-Euclidean geometry. I did not verify the idea; I should not have had time as, upon taking my seat in the omnibus, I went on with a conversation already commenced, but I felt a perfect certainty. Upon my return to Caen, for conscience' sake, I verified the result at my leisure." [*Poincare. 1913. P 387*]

Note that Poincare felt a sense of "perfect certainty" over the insight. This is typical of the "Aha!" moment. He believed in the knowledge and he set aside the problem of proving it until a later appropriate time. He also said that he was not consciously thinking about his mathematical work being distracted by the trip. The insight sprang upon him as if from out of the sky. He later deduced that his unconscious mind was probably teaming with activity over these matters. Within the context of tacit knowledge, we recognize that various subsidiary particulars were likely swarming around deep inside his brain and they suddenly integrated together forming a new focal comprehension. This insightful mental behavior was not a onetime event. Listen to his further descriptions:

"Then I turned my attention to the study of some arithmetical questions apparently without much success and without a suspicion of any connection with my preceding researches. Disgusted with my failure, I went to spend a few days at the seaside, and thought of something else. One morning, walking on the bluff, the idea came to me, with just the same characteristics of brevity, suddenness, and immediate certainty, that the arithmetic transformations of indeterminate ternary quadratic were identical with those of non-Euclidean geometry." (Poincare, 1913)

The description of the next event includes another interval of time occurring during a break from the rigors of mathematical analysis. During that downtime, another inspiration hit as if from the iconic bolt of lightning. Another "difficulty" soon obsessed his mind and:

"Thereupon I left for Mont-Valerein, where I was to go through my military service; so I was very differently occupied. One day, going along the street, the solution of the difficulty which had stopped me suddenly appeared to me. I did not try to go deep into it immediately, and only after my service did I again take up the question. I had all the elements and had only to arrange them and put them together. So I wrote out my final memoir at a single stroke and without difficulty (*Poincare, 1913. P. 388*)"

Let us pause and recognize that we as learners and teachers have a less demanding integration task in that discoveries made by geniuses, like Poincare, are being accomplished for the first time.

We as learners, however, encounter the task of integrating subsidiary particulars that are already chosen and offered to us in an organized fashion. The logical gap, however, sometimes as daunting as the Grand Canyon, still exists for us as well as for the original discoverer.

I stumbled across a description of John Fitch's sudden idea for the first steamboat. He struggled with the problem of transferring steam energy into some form of paddling and got nowhere. In exasperation and depression, he ran to the local tavern drowning his self-recriminations of failure in drink. He stumbled home the following night collapsing in bed at midnight. About an hour later, "The idea struck me about cranks and paddles for rowing a boat and for fear that I should lose the idea, I got up about 1 o'clock, struck a light and drew up the plan. I was so excited I could not sleep." Six days later, he demonstrated the first operating steamboat. (Bullock, 1905)

Up to this point I have highlighted the essential elements of Polanyi's tacit theory of knowledge. Do not think our detective work is done because much of the description of tacit integration is not found in the psychological research literature. More clues are needed to gain greater assurance that the process of a tacit integration, as pictured here, is not just a crazy fantasy. I will offer now a description of how I applied the theory of tacit knowledge to a practical educational problem. This example concerning the problem of floating and sinking objects is typically found within state standards for elementary school science. Once again the point here is not to cover a particular scientific topic but instead to offer it up as an example of how to apply the tacit theory of knowledge to the instructional design for meeting a curricular requirement.

An Example from Physical Science

A brilliant Greek mathematician, scientist, and engineer, Archimedes lived several hundred years BC in Syracuse, Sicily. Very little is known about his life but the story of how King Hiero II needed to judge if a crown was really made from gold is told by Marcus Vitruvius Pollio, a Roman soldier/architect in his book on architecture. Apparently, there was a story circulating at the time claiming the crown maker added silver into the mix allowing some gold to be deliberately withheld for the personal gain of the crown maker. The King needed proof of the deception yet desired not to melt down the crown for making the necessary measurements. He turned to Archimedes for help. While soaking at the baths, Archimedes noticed how the water rose in the tub as he immersed himself in it. Recognizing suddenly the significance of this observation, Archimedes allegedly jumped from the bath and ran home stark naked yelling "Eureka" (I have found it out). Archimedes weighed the crown. Then he prepared a chunk of gold with the same weight as the crown and another chunk of silver also having the same weight as the crown. He placed each of these chunks into vessels filled to the brim with water. The amount of water displaced was not the same showing the crown was not made of pure gold.

Different experimental approaches can demonstrate Archimedes principle but we note here how a tacit integration apparently took place in the mind of Archimedes offering to him the necessary understanding to solve the kings' puzzle. We know not what happened to the fraudulent crown maker.

The crown story leads us to a question that is typically part of science standards for elementary school students:

Why do some things sink and others float?

Children will offer up a variety of explanations such as:

- Heavy things sink (metal is heavy so it sinks)
- Light things float (wood is light hence it floats)
- Things float if they have air in them (balloons have air in them and they float on water)

Elementary teachers have other examples of student explanations to add to this list. However, these ideas usually do not count as "the explanation." Look in the official textbook and find that different things sink or float according to *"Archimedes principle"* Here we find a definition that goes something like this:

Any solid lighter than a fluid will, if placed in the fluid, be so far immersed that the weight of the solid will be equal to the weight of the fluid displaced.

(Heath, 1897)

Now we have "covered" Archimedes principle and can check the success of this learning experience with a test question whereby the student is asked to regurgitate the words back in the same order thus giving the appearance of their knowing Archimedes principle. If the state science standards specify that the student can explain why some things sink and others float, we allow the textbook to make a claim that the standard was covered based on the presence of a formal definition of Archimedes principle found on page such and such. But do all members of the class really *understand* anything? Often the formal textbook presentation is too glib and fails to help the reader form a comprehension of the topic. Missing from the simple reading exercise is anything like a period of struggle with dismay and distress where explanations were coupled with demonstrations of things actually sinking and floating. Do the learners know what "weight" means? How about the meaning of "fluid displaced?" Full understanding of Archimedes Principle requires integrating together all the various subsidiary particulars. These include weight, length, width, height, (leading to volume), while at the same time juggling the observed increase in water level within a container in which an object is floating or sinking. Then there is the observation that some floating objects float high and others are practically drowned, and so on.

To experience a tacit integration of all these subsidiary particulars, the student must know what these individual particulars mean. If they have not yet formulated an understanding of volume then the full understanding of Archimedes principle cannot take place. This is why formal education necessarily requires a carefully organized structure, ordering things that need to be understood before other things can be presented. Since all learners are different and bring to the table a vast array of different prior experiences and beliefs, the teacher has an even greater task in judging the considerable range of prior experiences found among members of the class. Instructional designs must therefore allow for differing levels of prior exposure, hence understanding, of these subsidiary particulars.

When old Archimedes made his insightful discovery his mind had to jump the same gap that any child must do today. We lose sight of this amazing feature of learning. Archimedes rightfully is famous for bridging the gap first. His name is appropriately attached to the discovery for all time, but every day in classrooms all over the planet, learners of all ages are trying to come to grips with the reason why some things float and others sink and must make that *same internal leap* that Archimedes did. No wonder the moment is full of such excitement and satisfaction. We all make the same discoveries hence passing along the great triumphs of human intellect.

One of the movements in science education unknowingly aimed at addressing the peculiar characteristics of tacit knowledge is called **inquiry instruction**. In the case of Archimedes Principle, students are given opportunities to conduct hands-on experiences with floating and sinking objects. If these experiences are sufficiently comprehensive and quantitative, there should be an increased likelihood for moments of tacit integration to occur. Let us look at how this learning process might occur in a school setting.

Archimedes Principle Instruction [an example]

Individual particulars need to be identified, examined, experienced, and understood. Start with rectangular blocks of various materials in different sizes. Students are offered these blocks along with measuring devices. Lengths, widths, and heights are measured. Volumes are then calculated. Volumes of many different sized blocks are compared with standard blocks such as cubic centimeters, cubic inches, or even a cubic foot. Give students other unmeasured blocks and ask them to **guess** the volume, followed by actual measurements. Then calculate the actual volume. Compare the guess with the calculation. Establishing a tacit sense of volume is strengthened through opportunities to look at different blocks, first guessing the amount of volume observed, then followed by checking the guess with measurements and calculations. Adding the guessing game into an experience with volume extends the instruction beyond a mere academic lab exercise (ok, I measured the blocks, am I done? Can I go now?). Offering only a few blocks and associated guessing is not likely to be enough exposure. Considerable repetition (practice) is needed to convert particulars into *subsidiary* particulars! Incidentally, a recent blog highlighted the complaint of an incensed reader when he saw guessing included as part of an instructional sequence in the "common core." The very idea of guessing anything seemed to the complainer to be an example of how awful new educational practices seem to be. Here is an example where the tacit theory of knowledge offers aid to those who fail to understand the full range of educational experiences needed for a complete pedagogy. Of course, learning is never about *only* guessing. Instructional strategies must offer a complete range of experiences that include real, hard work practicing the individual particulars until a full tacit integration is accomplished. There is no easy route to genuine comprehension and that includes skill development, which requires practice. The guessing example illustrates commonly held perceptions that teachers do not know what they are doing and that educational theory is nonsense.

Let us return to the problem of comprehending Archimedes principle. The subsidiary particular of "weight" has a number of complex issues embedded within it and some we choose to bypass such as the difference between the measuring of mass versus identifying weight as the force of gravity acting on the mass. Get around this by using units of force as the direct measurement of weight. A spring balance is the best way to integrate weight as a subsidiary particular. Weight is a measure of the force that the earth exerts on an object (that force is itself mysterious and is typically accepted from years of prior experience by the student). Blocks weighed using a spring balance offer a direct visceral cue that measurements are being caused by the tug of the earth on the block. Metal blocks of the same size as wooden blocks show up, as expected, to be heavier than wood. Then a wrinkle shows up when some small metal blocks have a lower weight than other larger wooden blocks (Is it possible to get a metal block small enough to float?) Instructional experiences should offer opportunities to make guesses about how much some of the blocks weigh. Guessing forces the learner to **indwell** in the characteristic under examination. Also good questions may erupt from the mind first coming to grips with the content. Taking the opportunity to follow up on these naturally occurring questions is highly desirable.

All key subsidiary particulars for Archimedes principle are hopefully planted into the learners mind with sufficient strength to be of later use. Unfortunately, some students are saddled with previously acquired misconceptions that are incorrect (a barrier to integration). The teacher must offer enough exercises to allow observation of student beliefs and responses. Further directed questioning is employed to uncover and correct the misconception thereby allowing installation of a corrected concept. For example, how about that vague "displacement" word when describing a fluid being pushed out of the way by a floating or sinking object? Go back to the real world, fill a cup to the very top with water, and let a block of wood settle into the cup. Water clearly flows out of the cup. This observation shows that water is pushed out of the way when something like a block is allowed to settle into it. If the cup is not filled to the brim one can still see a heightened level of water when the block is lowered into the cup. These observations should be enough to clarify the meaning of *displaced*. Now, how much water is displaced? Capture the overflow water and weigh it. This weight is then compared to the weight of the block and found to be roughly the same (to the degree that measurement uncertainty allows). Do this enough times and a learner may come to believe that the weight of the displaced water is the same as the entire weight of the floating block.

All of this carefully organized information is logically sufficient for some minds to create the desired understanding of Archimedes principle. However not all brains work alike and despite  the care used to design and present all the necessary information and experiences, not everyone will immediately leap across the gap and "get it"! Such is the nature of learning when different students are confronted with instructional strategies. In fact some well-prepared minds may not even need to conduct any experiments at all or watch any of these live demonstrations. They may already know enough to jump the conceptual gap the first time around by only reading the full description in a book. On the other hand despite the careful experiential and logical instructional design, some learners may falter; the puzzled look is maintained on a disappointed face. This leads to some unfortunate side effects such as internalized feelings that science is an undesirable topic or the learner develops some self-loathing about being just too "stupid" to do this stuff. Other consequences may include hiding the failure such as bravely trying to pretend that they do understand it (especially if the teacher is eager to believe such subterfuge). Patience, elapsed "simmering time", and repetition of experiences are needed in these cases along with freedom from ridicule. Sheila Tobias in a seminal book (*Overcoming Math Anxiety*) talks about the common resistance to mathematics found in schools today. Her ideas are directly applicable to science as well. She denigrates the idea that some persons are not mathematically inclined hence should not bother trying to learn it. Her discussion on intuition is especially relevant to what is being said here. If you have not read her book I urgently recommend that you do so! (Tobias, 1978).

Throughout science and mathematics the presence of a memorized formula along with an apparent ability to crank out correct answers using the formula, is too often a crutch that hides the lack of real tacit comprehension of a concept. We want and need to achieve that sublime moment of the "Aha!" of deep understanding. The example described above has so many measurements and displacements under differing conditions that confusion is a major danger. I have carefully gone through these exercises with classrooms of students all the while sensing that everyone seemed to understand what was going on. Several days later, when coming back to the topic, I found that some of the participants forgot either what was done or never really did "indwell" in the experiences. One cannot assume that a topic or subsidiary particular has been covered adequately. I agree with the use of regular short quizzes as diagnostic devices to judge the progress of the learner (formative testing).

After comprehension is achieved, the learner is in a good position to try out the newly acquired knowledge with problem solving. Simple plug-in-the-numbers type problems may offer some limited ideas about how well students have coped with the instructional materials. But the judgment of real understanding depends upon the use of problems that have unusual quirks or twists to them forcing serious thinking and application of what we now hope is true comprehension of the subject matter. These kinds of problems typically give rise to complaints that they are "not fair", we "did not cover that"! This complaint indicates that learners do not understand the nature of comprehension. I also want to point out that, at first glance, objective tests may seem to be mechanistic and cannot test true understanding. This is not true; it's all about the skill of the test writer. Some objective tests are very limited in what they measure but others can be quite sophisticated.

Tacit Knowledge is Not Just Found In Science

So by now you think I am only interested in applying tacit knowledge to science. That thought comes naturally because physics is my academic field but the tacit theory of knowledge works in all areas and endeavors. For example one of the challenges facing the elementary teacher is the problem of reading. Already mentioned is the tacit component to reading, which refers to shifting mental effort away from the laborious construction of words from letters and then the slow combination of words into sentences. That process needs to become tacit in order for the mind to direct attention to the meaning expressed by the sentences. Apparently, it does not even end there. How many times have we, typically in a state of exhaustion or under conditions of worry, discovered that we just read a paragraph without any idea of what we had just read? Learners fall into the same trap while studying the textbook or at early stages of learning to read. Harvey and Goudvis (Harvey & Goudvis, 2007) wrote a book offering a number of strategies for helping the new reader move beyond the stage of just running through the words without actively absorbing the meaning of what they are referencing. I was initially disconcerted by their expressed wish to move readers up from the lowest level of reading which they called "tacit reader" to the advanced level of being a "reflective reader." Hey, wait a moment, isn't tacit the highest level of comprehension? Well, when referring to the beginning reader they seem to be recognizing that it takes tacit knowledge to go from letters to words to sentences but then we need the reader to pass beyond that meaning of a tacit process to constructing comprehension of the entire passage being read. To accomplish this they offer a number of strategies for the reader to employ such as visualization, asking questions, making inferences, and connecting the material in the book to something personal in their own lives. That all makes good sense and just goes to show how much there is to teaching reading.

Music is an obvious application of tacit knowledge but the need for endless practice is so well known that a danger exists in replacing this entire book with a simple exhortation to just practice and eventually you get "it." Polanyi offers a structure for understanding comprehension that explains the higher purpose of practice; developing tacit skill leading to tacit integrations. Practice is certainly centrally important, but an appreciation for the structure of tacit knowledge adds richness to understanding the need for practice and what is accomplished when you do it. Practicing the performance of any physical skill looks obvious enough but when the skill area is cognitive (mental) the practice shows up in repetitive examination of various explanations for something hard to understand. Practicing is a bad word in some current educational methodologies; I use the term here to mean repetition of review of the various particulars that make up a complex idea. Mulling something over in the mind to gain ultimately a tacit integration, hence the "Aha!" experience is a form of practice and is necessary and good. On the other hand endless drill on the use of some procedure might be reasonably questioned under some circumstances.

Music appreciation does not rely exclusively on practicing an instrument but instead is based upon having sufficient experiential exposure to music to create an emotional response to it. Symphony orchestras are lately experiencing a crisis of audience development. Today's youth are not responding to the music of the great masters because they are not sufficiently exposed to the music needed to build a tacit integration of the subsidiary particulars making up that music. This is a shame; those who are missing the experience do not know what they are missing.

These examples exemplifying the use of tacit knowledge in education only touch the surface. But by now you should have a good notion about what the theory of tacit knowledge really is. Digging deeper will now uncover yet more clues into how tacit knowledge works as the detective gets closer to understanding how all this fits into educational practice.

Chapter Three: Learning and Teaching

How can I put this understanding of tacit knowledge to use? For the sake of the teacher and learner we now examine educational practice (pedagogy) looking for clues about how the theory of tacit knowledge illuminates educational practice.

No simple recipe mixing tacit knowledge into the educational stew easily solves educational problems. Tacit based insights do exist and I have found over the years that the well-studied educational journey makes more sense when viewed from the perspective of tacit knowing. I will test Polanyi's theory of tacit knowledge by using it to derive best practices for learning and teaching. This is a process of logical deduction and assumes that all we have said about tacit knowledge is true. Not everyone in the academic community may agree but never mind about that yet; let's see where applications of tacit theory can take us!

Tacit Teaching and Learning

Look closely at the moment when the essence of learning takes place. The event we call tacit integration or *insight*. This is the instant when everything falls into place, and we recognize that finally we understand a puzzle of understanding, we "get it" and are exultant. Keep in mind that achieving integration is the desired outcome; hence, we ask this question: **how do we get there?** If only we had some quirky knobs sticking out from the back of our heads which, when turned just right, could dial up the "Aha!" experience.

Unfortunately, such knobs do not exist; even worse, there are no controllable mental knobs accessible to consciousness that can bring about the tacit integration. The experience we seek comes to us as if by *magic*. You can stare at the ceiling and squeeze your brain, pushing as hard as you can, but no integration occurs. You can wish, beg, cry, and have a fit but the integration just does not take place at your call on your schedule (and especially not on the schedule of a school!).

So, what do you do to learn?

Let us go back to review what is required for the integration. *First*: You need to have available inside your mind all of those various particulars (pieces and parts) making up the whole thing that you desire to understand. *Second*: These pieces need to be known in a **subsidiary** **manner** in order for focal awareness to jump over the logical gap to the "promised land" where everything comes together. Those little particulars need to be **in your brain** and they need to be there in a useful form, on the periphery of consciousness so that, at the right moment, when you look away, lightning strikes. The mind cannot do its unconscious magic if "the line is busy" while you are stuck processing the thoughts using focal concentration upon each individual particular. That kind of focus (practice), while necessary, interferes with looking at all the parts in a subsidiary manner. *Third:* we might need downtime, sometimes we need periods of *incubation* where the conscious brain wanders off to irrelevant thoughts and settles upon irrelevant things. Mindless activity seems to be a good way to vacate the premises, such as mowing the yard, washing dishes, jogging, painting the window frame, enjoying recess (note: recess is good for learning), in fact any sort of work or play where you have some opportunity to engage the mind in a limited sense without exhaustion. Unfortunately, this simmering time is difficult to arrange in the setting of formal education where the clock forces learning to take place on the institutional schedule. The organizational reality of formal education puts elapsed time ahead of mastering comprehension. Thus, we end up stuck with speed-of-learning as an unfortunate variable when evaluating student performance, and in too many cases, the time allotted is not sufficient for tacit integration to take place.

In his comprehensive biography of Einstein, Walter Isaacson reports on the observations of Einstein's son Hans who described his father's use of violin playing when stuck on a problem resisting solution. After a while, Einstein would exultantly stop playing with an expression of satisfaction due to some sudden insight thus solving the problem (Isaacson, 2008). The description is clearly an example of incubation at work followed by the tacit integration that we now recognize as the flash of insight.

Another example surfaces among the series of mysteries penned by Sir Arthur Conan Doyle where Sherlock Holmes sometimes categorized the difficulty of a problem in terms of how many pipes of puffing it took before an answer appeared to his consciousness. Perhaps Holmes indwelled within the subsidiary particulars while Watson contented himself cogitating upon the outward focal knowledge of the case

Incubation time vs immersion

Fourth: The incubation time does not accomplish much unless the learner brings to it deep **immersion** in all modalities of exposure to the subject. The downtime referred to above is only effective if content is boiling away inside the brain - content existing from prior immersion in all aspects of the issue being studied. Reading different books and articles on the subject, listening to explanations, talking to others, perhaps watching videos and having direct experiences with the content all provide raw material for the mind to chew upon during incubation. Unfortunately, nobody can predict how much time the mind will need to work over the material accessed. This is why that moment of tacit integration is such a surprise and so welcome. Closely related to immersion is the need for the learner to be focused on the task, to really want to succeed, to be **fully engaged** (*fifth* requirement but not in the order presented). The word *grit* is now used within educational circles to describe this feature of learning. If learners fully understood what behaviors are needed to bring about full comprehension, measurable educational success is likely to increase to the satisfaction of all involved.

Despite a need for these features to be present so that comprehension can occur, a scheduled period of incubation is not always helpful. You could be missing some unrecognized bit of information essential for the integration or worse you may be stuck with a subsidiary particular that happens to be incorrect (another barrier). These faulty elements are called *misconceptions* that block integration from taking place. The "whole" to which you need to be focally directed requires a coherent and correct pattern of subsidiary particulars. If you are saddled with something in error, then the information in your mind cannot fit together, is not coherent, and the brain is unable to form a tacit integration. Curiously several competing coherent wholes might exist at the same time allowing subsidiary particulars to form wholes with contrasting results. For example, look at one of the famous drawings that flip your consciousness back and forth between two different and contrasting representations (Weisstein).

The subsidiary particulars in this image can cohere together in two entirely different ways. One visual effect offers to our awareness the image of an old woman looking downward and to her left while the other perspective shows a young woman looking away from the viewer to her right. You cannot see these two representations *at the same moment.* Flipping between the two images requires changing the tacit integration. When seen for the first time a

viewer tends to "see" one of the women and that perceived image blocks the ability to see the other. In the same manner when a belief that you hold about some subsidiary particular is especially strong it can force a tacit integration which is not the desired one and we end up with a rigid misconception interfering with learning. Switching for the first time from one woman to the other is an insight moment and we suddenly exclaim with amazement that we see the other image. This perspective shift comes about from a different tacit integration leading to a moment of new insight. The switch from one woman to the other happens all at once and completely. You do not sneak up gradually on the other image although, once seen, you can employ focused attention to *analyze* how a specific subsidiary particular is used to achieve the desired effect (for example, the old women eye is the young woman's ear).

How can you know when a subsidiary particular is missing or another one is wrong?

Try explaining what you know to someone else. Perhaps you suspect that something is missing or wrong. By exposing the contents of your mind to others, you have a chance to find out from them what the missing piece is or if something is in error. They might catch it or they may not. In a classroom setting this is simply called asking the teacher for help or talking to a classmate. This feature of learning is aided through what has become known as "collaborative learning" where a small group of learners talks to each other. I have found that referring to a number of different books helps because one of them may say something different in just the right way offering clarification about a point not fully grasped.

While waiting for the insight moment, learners need opportunities for incubation time, accompanied by a repeated return to the search. Immersion followed by incubation followed by immersion and so forth; it goes back and forth. Act like a dog on a walk, seeking, always sniffing, looking, actively engaged in grasping at everything within reach, hoping for a bone left in an unexpected place - the bone that unlocks the puzzle and sends you to that desired flash of insight.

A fascinating research study into the underlying structure of insight points to one of the ways our minds interfere with the necessary integration. When confronting a learning puzzle, our brain searches within a "representation space," composed of the set of subsidiary particulars that – as imposed upon us through experiences -- seem to us to be relevant and have a connection to one another. Here is an example. Suppose we are shown a simple formula using Roman numerals like this one:

$$IV = III - I$$

The statement is incorrect. Four is certainly not three minus one. Transform the symbolic representation into physical reality by mapping this arrangement on a tabletop using matchsticks. Your task is now to make the formula correct by moving *one* matchstick to a different place. We exert considerable focal effort while trying to make one of the numbers different by shifting a matchstick from one location to another. Solvers are pre-programmed (fixated) to expect that the problem solution require changing the value of a number because that is how we learned to do mathematics. We become stuck in this *representation space* (another barrier) and search around in *that* space for the answer. We fail, become frustrated, and leave the problem to seek incubation time.

Solving this problem requires changing the representation space to something different. How about forgetting the value of the numbers and, instead, think about the mathematical operation? The problem includes an equals sign and a minus sign. We do not normally play around with the mathematical operations because in a math problem those operations are there to accomplish a desired calculation; changing them is abnormal. However, the initial task never asked you to maintain the arithmetical operation at all! If one of the equals sign matchsticks were to be moved from its location and transferred over to the minus sign we get the following:

$$IV - III = I$$

Instantly correct! The representation space had to be shifted to allow thinking in a different way (called *restructuring* by cognitive psychologists). This research study went beyond just measuring the restructuring effect. It cleverly showed that the idea of shifting perspectives occurred through **unconscious processing** rather than from conscious analytical thought; further evidence that tacit integrations are accomplished through the behavior of something mental happening subconsciously (Ash & Wiley, 2006).

Value of explicit or direct instruction

The elaborate process leading to tacit integration sounds difficult, chancy, and debilitating. Happily what you are aiming for is not always so terribly difficult to reach. At the beginning of the journey, you may be pleased to find that initial immersion in the details of a problem is sufficient. What I am trying to say is that tacit integration, for some people, can pop out of an appropriate offering of explicit knowledge. Never denigrate the value and significance of explicit learning whether delivered verbally or in written form. Sometimes called "**direct instruction**," learning offers that which we can articulate symbolically and only sometimes may require augmentation with tacit inputs. Depending upon prior knowledge and experiences, some learners will achieve the gap-crossing event with a simple exposure to explicit instruction, hence building their repertoire with new understandings. It is the more difficult issues that may need repeated application of seeking, immersion, and incubation to gain completion of the tacit integration. The full repertoire of necessary information includes prior knowledge and experience of the learner as well as offerings from a teacher and other sources. Consider as well the possibility that comprehension does not always occur in a sudden tacit integration. Understanding can sneak up on the effortful mind and you gradually realize that you have just figured it out.

Tacit Teaching

The other side of our effort to acquire a tacit integration is the related problem of being the teacher to a student who seeks to form a tacit integration. Judging from the theory already described, the teacher has an especially difficult task. Merely offering up explicit instruction, while part of the need to fill a student's mind with subsidiary particulars, is typically not enough to help them reach that final understanding of a tacit integration. Step one for a student, is to grasp the idea of tacit knowledge itself so *they* realize what needs to happen. Prospective teachers study theories of learning and instruction but rarely explain to the students themselves what actions need to be taken! If you, as a student, do not understand the elements of how effective understandings are acquired, how can you be expected to behave accordingly? I recall my own teachers telling the class to take good notes, study by rewriting them for homework, read the textbook, solve problems if appropriate, but never a peep about aiming for tacit integrations. The single most important contribution of a student is the decision to get involved, to pay attention, to engage in the material needed to form a tacit integration. They must understand the gap is crossed by themselves in their own minds and not put there by the teacher.

This misunderstanding about education offers them an excuse to slide by, to disengage, to merely cram for a test, and in all other ways decide not to learn. **How to explain the theory of tacit knowledge to a learner is an unexamined challenge in education today.**

Published suggestions on how an instructor can guide tacit instruction are not readily found in the literature. The educational establishment has not embraced Polanyi, in fact seems not to be aware of his existence or his ideas. Nicholas Burbules, a practicing philosopher, serves as an example of an explicator of tacit teaching. He recognized that a famous philosopher, Wittgenstein, taught in a manner best described as "Tacit Teaching." Searching for common elements of a Wittgenstein teaching style - based on his belief that limits exist to how much can be directly explicated - Burbules compiled recollections of Wittgenstein's students (Burbules, 2008). Wittgenstein "showed" rather than "said." He modeled thought processes for students to observe, imitate, and try out in a trial and error manner subject to his correction. Expectations that students should do the thinking led to long periods of silence described as painful. As a teacher myself, I typically feel a persistent need to keep the airwaves chattering with sound. This practice is comforting because it is how I learned how teachers covered content. Yet sometimes the learner needs to have quiet time for reflection. Often the guide needs to slow down, be patient, and let the learner alone to cogitate in silence. We older teachers exhibit a nearly desperate need to talk, to explain, to lecture, to explicate when all we accomplish is to keep the learners mind passively occupied with focal input instead of allowing time to incubate what already exists.

Wittgenstein was concerned about confusions he believed the students possessed without anyone identifying these misconceptions. He proposed thought experiments for the class to think about and discuss and chose to openly expose his own uncertainties and confusions concerning critical ideas. This behavior is in contrast to the teacher as the all-knowing expert whose pronouncements are to be taken as authoritative truth. A review of Wittgenstein's approach to teaching is indeed revealing.

Teachers know that not everyone in a classroom setting is fully engaged in the activities needed for attaining true understanding of a complex subject. Students who mindlessly go through the motions of learning without paying attention simply will not get there. Memorizing disjointed facts in order to pass a test will fail to offer the necessary exposure to all the subsidiary particulars needed to experience the "Aha!" moment. As the old adage points out, horses led to water may not drink. Learners must want to learn and must be fully engaged and fully attentive, or else the mind does not have enough focus to gather up the necessary particulars and absorb them to the point a tacit integration is possible. The various particulars needed to form an understanding must be present or the whole will not form; these particulars have to be processed by the mind into a *subsidiary* manner in order to cohere thus allowing the formation of a tacit integration. The learner has to bring themselves to the table. No surprise here but the structure of tacit knowing makes the need for deliberative attention quite clear. Books exist on the subject of motivation so meeting this need will not be addressed further here.

Fads in education

Educators are subject to all manner of claims about how certain types of pedagogy should be recognized as the most effective (hence denigrating others that have not been blessed by the claimant). If we have learned anything from the pattern we call tacit knowledge, it is recognition of the value of all modalities of learning. The juxtaposition of all instructional strategies working together, nudge the learner over the fearsome gap, thus triggering a tacit integration. We hear complaints in the press about the faddishness of education; I suggest that a pedagogical technique is identifiable as a fad when its adherents insist their sacred approach is the best and only appropriate approach to use. On the contrary, the pattern we see in tacit knowledge shows why *all* modalities of learning have their place and, hence, offer no evidence of being a fad. In his delightful book *Permission to Forget,* Lee Jenkins talks about the swinging of educational pendulums as schools go back and forth between emphases on one teaching approach to another. Pendulum warfare stress hits teachers from one side of the head to the other - all without would-be combatants ever noticing that student learning is where the focus needs to be placed (Jenkins, 2005). Even my caution about not memorizing facts should be placed into context. Sometimes the memorized facts may serve as raw particulars needed for later formation of the tacit integration. Do not get stuck on the rules.

Who is in control?

In some limited applications, a rigid and carefully controlled set of instructional steps (as found in computer programmed instruction) has some value. We must bear in mind that straitjacketing teaching materials has the disadvantage of blocking access to the learners' own pre-existing knowledge or to a specific modality of experience that would be ideal for the learner at that moment. Those who are trying to understand something complicated need control over the sequence and pacing and modality of content. What is right for one person may hit at the wrong moment for someone else. James B Conant said there is always the first time one reads Mobay Dick and then there is the *right* time. Happily, there is a new modern twist to the old programmed instruction craze that hit many decades ago. This approach is called **adaptive learning** and takes advantage of new, astounding computer power and associated databases to judge when a student is having difficulty and then programmatically offer that student carefully prepared and appropriate remediation.

Computers are necessarily programmed. The adaptive part means computers do a great deal more than offer simple saved presentations of information on a computer screen. Test questions are offered on a regular basis to check on the progress made by the student. Depending on the kinds of answers received, the computer identifies what specific problems a learner has and selects additional instructional information to help the student move forward or overcome misconceptions. Some adaptive systems rely on capturing the experiences of many students and can incorporate knowledge gained from these collective experiences. In this manner, an adaptive system begins to behave like a human tutor offering just the right information to the student at the right moment. Because of this apparent replacement of a live teacher, the adaptive model gives rise to a strong pushback from educators who sense a threat to their jobs as well as a doubt that computers can truly be as effective as a real instructor would be. The growing number of companies developing adaptive systems is triggering complaints that industry is merely seeking another arena for extracting profits. In the long run this technology will be successful (or not) depending on how effective the computer can act like a tutor and how well costs are driven lower based on wide-spread use of the systems. Regardless of the value offered by adaptive systems we will always need the live judgement of a skilled and caring teacher.

Another practical example of a tacit teaching style is found in the writings of Dr. Henry S. Gurr, retired professor of physics from the University of South Carolina, Aiken. I encourage the reader to go to his excellent website to review directly what he has learned over many years of teaching and coaching students (Gurr, 2008).

Gurr calls his system DART (Discover and Resolve Tutoring). He developed DART from observations of student-coaching sessions during which he recorded and then analyzed the emotional reactions of learners. He noticed that a flash of insight was detectable when a student finally understood a resistant idea. Gurr called this moment a *discovery event* and systematically uncovered teacher and learner behaviors necessary to trigger that event (we call it tacit integration). He documented a ten-step process that usually led a student from being stuck to the desired insight moment. I will briefly summarize these steps here. Notice the elements of tacit theory embedded within his approach. The word "steps" suggests a sequential series of linear moves taken by the tutor, but in Gurr's system these are better recognized as a set of teacher behaviors occurring in a blended and sometimes parallel manner.

Gurr begins after some form of instruction has taken place (lecture, textbook readings, etc.) but the student is stuck where the information does not hang together. **The first step** in Gurr's system consists of the student asking for help. Gurr claims that further teacher talk at this point is not helpful. Let the student do the talking. This is a "show me" time allowing the coach to infer what is happening in the students mind. Encourage as much information flow as possible from student to teacher. In Polanyian terms imagine the teacher trying to deduce which subsidiary particulars exist inside the mind of the student. In **step two** Gurr asks the teacher to focus attention on student behavior as the information flow proceeds. Interpret bodily language and eye movements and especially be on the lookout (**step three**) for strong emotional signs of distress, possibly requiring the end of the session. Gurr is concerned that being stuck can be confounded with emotional problems extending beyond the classroom. These need to be addressed before proceeding further with the educational objectives (seeking a counselors help is sometimes appropriate). Anxiety can come from the frustration of cognitive hang up, and thus, the teacher needs to offer support and understanding, with the goal to gain release of this tension. As the session continues in **step four**, the coach asks the student various leading questions to gain ideas about where the student is stuck. The questioning demonstrates a desire to know what the student is thinking and feeling (you can rely on emotion as an avenue to the subconscious where subsidiary particulars are trying to integrate together). This sort of discussion is intended to strengthen the student's sense of self-worth by having the student do the talking and explaining. In **step five** the coach offers encouragement, hence making the session as pleasant as possible. The coach should avoid Interruptions, negative feedback, and evidence of frustration as well as actions that put the student on the spot (being "on stage" leads to further cognitive blockage). The student may need to develop improved study habits, so in **step six** the guide offers subtle reinforcement of good habits yet without forceful exhortations to do better or to pay better attention (even though these behaviors are desirable, it's best for the student to figure this out based on clues offered by the coach).

Step seven repeats a warning to the teacher to avoid taking over flooding the student with fresh detailed explanations through more lecturing. Gurr considers directed teacher behavior to be counterproductive because it just "piles on more words" and presumes the instructor knows what the student needs to hear (not possible since the manner in which a student's thinking can go awry is unpredictable). Under these circumstances the student may nod in agreement as if to say, "yes I follow you, I understand (I'm not dumb)" while still drowning in confusion and uncertainty.

Step eight aims at the heart of the problem. what information is missing or what erroneous particulars are blocking integration? This is why the instructor must listen carefully in order to draw out information from the student to diagnose what is wrong. Eventually the nature of the problem becomes clear yet the path forward is still problematic. In **step nine** the teacher finally aims the student in the right direction without explicitly explaining the problem. The learner needs to discover the block by attending to some form of "pointing" from the teacher (Wittgenstein was a pointer). Let us go on a side trip for a moment and then we will come back to finish DART.

What's so funny?

Gurr has cleverly explored how understanding a joke exhibits the same underlying structure as trying to comprehend something not initially obvious. Suppose you were asked a silly question such as: "how do you get down from an elephant?" The receiver of the joke thinks a little, imagines a ladder, but really just wants to hear the punch line so they ask, "how?" The answer is: "You don't get down from an elephant; you get down from a duck!" Blank stare - so what is the joke?

Some folks might get it after a while, but others do not. A joke is a problem of tacit integration. Until you "get it" or "understand it" the joke falls flat. The joke teller can act like a tacit teacher and ask for information from the frustrated listener such as:

"what are you thinking about"? The listener may describe imagining climbing down from a quacking duck but the image does not work because ducks are so small you do not get *down* from them as you would from an elephant. Instead of explaining the joke the teacher does a better job by pointing to the disconnection. Suppose the joke teller simply hints: "wrong kind of down." Now the receiver has a chance to restructure what they internalized as the meaning of duck, the meaning of "down," and then realize the kind of *down* being considered is present under the feathers of the duck. That switch in perspective can bring about a laugh if crazy enough; in this case the joke is too lame but does illustrate the underlying mechanism at work. The student does not initially comprehend the joke because a subsidiary particular is the wrong one, hence blocking the tacit integration. Notice how the joke teller need not explain the joke; instead, the teller just points to the source of the confusion and allows the listener to make an internal shift in meaning. This tactic allows the joke to make sense. This internal shift in meaning was met earlier when dealing with the Roman numeral problem. There is a needed change in the representation space, a shift that changes the relationship among subsidiary particulars so that they can integrate successfully. Jokes are effective in illustrating the structure of tacit knowledge and the formation of a tacit integration. Examples of visual illusions do the same thing when flipping back and forth between two utterly different ways of seeing.

Back to DART: **Step ten** is the resulting flash of insight thus completing the task of comprehension.

Another mode of instruction, similar to tutoring, is the ancient master/apprentice relationship that over many centuries served to transmit skillful performance. Gamble studied the relationship among cabinetmakers in South Africa and noticed how minor a role symbolic verbal explanation played in the transmission of cabinetmaking skill. The details of the craft were passed along through the demonstration and modeling of behavior. Drawings served as the most explicit part of instruction, yet even when presented with drawings, apprentices had to absorb their meaning with minimal help. Gamble described the characteristics of this training by using tacit knowledge as the framework; masters judged performance on such vague observations as the bodily stance of the apprentice, the unique sound his tools made, and the manner in which jigs were constructed and positioned. Attempts to convert the master/apprentice instruction into abstract classroom based training left out critical pieces of skill development (subsidiary awareness of performance detail) (Gamble, 2001). These cues help our detective work as we continue to uncover the meaning and application of tacit knowledge to the teaching/learning situation.

Stages of problem solving

Hubert Dreyfus (philosopher) and Stuart Dreyfus (engineering) offer a different categorization of understanding in their 1986 book, *Mind over Machine: The Power of Human Intuition and Expertise in the Era of the Computer* (Dreyfus & Dreyfus, 1986). They were responding to a movement in education that saw in the computer a new frontier for modeling the teaching of concepts, how to think, as well as offering an artificial replacement of mental cognition through artificial intelligence. In their view, a distinction is needed between "knowing that" vs. "knowing how." The same distinction is found in the current psychological literature between "declarative knowledge" vs. "procedural knowledge." If the kind of knowledge that you have is explicable in symbolic form, you can *declare* the information and can claim to "know that." On the other hand, if the knowledge is *procedural* in character, you "know how" but do not necessarily have the communicative tools to explain what it is that you can do. The parallels with focal and tacit knowing are obvious if not identical. Dreyfus and Dreyfus proceeded to build a **five stage learning process** showing how a learner moves from novice to expert. Their thinking was based on the capability of computers to mimic, echo, or replace humans in these steps. Their staging is not the same as Gurr's DART system described earlier. Now we focus, instead, upon identifying stages of learning aimed at leading to the comprehension of a complex concept and its application to problem solving effectiveness. We should be able to recognize the tacit knowledge pattern showing up in these stages.

Stage 1 Novice: – Fact Gathering and Rule Recognition

Fact gathering and rule recognition is the first step taken by the beginner. The use of these facts and rules requires focused attention on the part of the learner (Polanyi would identify focal awareness as operative at this stage). Physics students may memorize the equation for Newton's second law of motion, $F=MA$, and plug numbers into the equation to solve for the missing value. Novices do not have a broad understanding of dynamics at this point and can only follow the rule in a rudimentary and limited manner. Archimedes' principle is recognized as pertaining to floating and sinking and so novices can explicitly follow the algorithmic rules to calculate and then judge if a prescribed block of wood would float or sink. They are not likely to appreciate the links to other particulars involved nor have the explicated parts embedded in their mind in a subsidiary manner. The stage one learner is unlikely to solve problems requiring any deeper thought than rote plugging of numbers into known equations. They expect a test to ask them for this low level form of task completion and complain that anything more complex is unfair.

Stage 2 Advanced Beginner:-Collections of Experiences

The experience gained from repeated exposure to the facts and rules begins to exert some influence over the behavior of the learner. These collections of experiences are strengthened in value through additional verbal knowledge offered to the students. When applying Newton's laws of motion the learner begins to recognize more complex situations so that acceleration, rather than serving as just another number to plug into a memorized equation, may need to be calculated from basic kinematic information [a searching task that requires only focal attention from the learner]. This situation offers clues to the problem that novices miss in their limited and focused attention on the basic rules and facts. Perhaps a floating or sinking block of wood is about to be dunked into a container of oil, thus requiring redirection of attention to the density of oil being different from the density of water. How does that quirk affect the outcome of the analysis?

Stage 3 Competence:-Strategy of Approach

Problem solvers can now see the wider view of the issue in question and are able to work out a strategy of approach, hence using knowledge acquired up to this point in a somewhat creative manner. All the subsidiary particulars are recognized and employed. Notice that as we move along these stages, students' responses to an offered problem are used to judge what stage of knowledge the students have attained. We may ask at what point has the tacit integration taken place? When did the "Aha" moment occur? Considering that at this competence stage, cognition indicates awareness and understanding of the various subsidiary particulars, most likely integration is taking place in stage 3.

Stage 4 Proficiency:-Intuitions and Inference

The Dreyfus brothers mention intuition when describing the behavior of problem solvers. They understand intuition to be "the understanding that effortlessly occurs due to discriminations resulting from previous experiences" [p 28]. Uncovering what this intuition machine really is and its relationship to tacit knowledge will need further elaboration later; meanwhile, the Dreyfus' book takes care to eliminate intuition as an effect of simple guessing or the exhibition of a mysterious mystical communion with reality. The presence of an **inference**, not analytically (consciously) derived, is considered as an important attribute of the exercise of intuition in their scheme. Proficient performers are able to sort through features of the problem space without conscious deliberation and settle upon the most important and useful elements needed for problem resolution. Polanyi would recognize this behavior as the functioning of tacit knowledge working behind the scenes of direct consciousness.

Stage 5 Expertise:-Reflections on Intuitions

The performance of the expert is described not so much as the involvement of thinking but, instead, as the use of reflections upon intuitions. Deliberate and calculated analysis is replaced with nearly automated responses based on the associations connected to prior experience. As with the nature of tacit knowledge, if the mind reverts to focal attention, the skilled performance is broken.

I once enjoyed hosting the magician "The Amazing Randy" in a college physical science class (he takes considerable pains to show students that extrasensory claims are tricks and not founded on mystical powers). After some amazing feats of spoon bending and apparent mind reading, he mentioned to me later that much of what he does is automatic, and hence, he will not watch a video of himself performing magic tricks since that directs his attention onto the focal details of his performance, which is antithetical to smooth execution of the tricks. This revelation came up because in a classroom setting he could not be as prepared as in a stage show and had to adapt quickly to the circumstances before him. I was surprised how easily he handled the loose and open classroom setting before him including my presence behind the lab table in the front of the lecture hall. Much of that fluent behavior was due to expert performance operating in a tacit manner.

The Dreyfus brothers conclude that while information processing (analogous to computer models of human thought) may offer some degree of correspondence to analytical thinking, we need to value the intuitive side of human cognition as a distinctly different but highly valuable form of thought. Dreyfus and Dreyfus exhibit in their stages beliefs consistent with the tacit theory of knowledge.

At this point in the journey, we have pursued the development and understanding of the theory of tacit knowledge as applied to the practical problem of education. I offered some examples of how the tacit theory of knowledge is used in an educational setting and I hope this information is sufficient for the practitioner to try it out.

Chapter Four: Educational Psychology

I have mentioned my puzzlement that the insightful analysis offered by Michael Polanyi is not found in textbooks of educational psychology. Someone completing a BS degree in education at just about any college or university is likely to graduate without ever running across Polanyi's name or even a reference to tacit knowledge. I will not at this time reopen speculations as to why this state of affairs exists but, instead, will now compare what is known about tacit knowledge to what is found in the current research literature in educational psychology. Could the omission be due to a consensus view that Polanyi was wrong? We now take on this exploration with a shallow dive into contemporary research into cognitive psychology.

Where do we find references to tacit knowledge in published educational research?

The Two Sigma Problem

Henry Gurr is plowing a field previously studied by Benjamin Bloom who asked the central question about what constitutes best educational practices and posed what he called the "two sigma problem." Benjamin Bloom is famous for *Blooms Taxonomy*, a categorical system that sorted through various levels of cognitive complexity (more about that later). He is not as well known for a fascinating series of studies based on the proposition that one-on-one tutoring (exemplified by Gurr and the master/apprentice relationship studied by Gamble) is measurably the very best instructional strategy. The careful documentation of tutoring we just discussed with the help of Henry Gurr supports Blooms claim.

With the success of tutoring in mind, Bloom challenged the educational community to come up with new modes of group instruction that are as effective as tutoring. To understand his results, I offer to you in the first graph below an image showing what testing results look like for a large class - assuming simple lecturing and homework. Variation between different students in a test measurement is estimated by calculating the "standard deviation" for all the test results. Typically, most test data is found within 3 standard deviations on either side of the average grade.

Theoretical Grading Curve for a Class

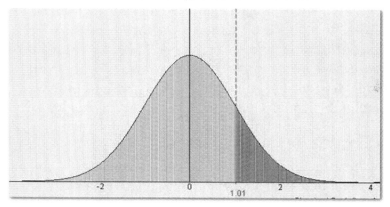

The solid line indicates the mean, the dotted line is located at one standard deviation above the mean

Blooms challenge recognized the impractical expense of any school system paying for one-on-one tutors for every student.

Research into this "one on one" form of instruction discovered that average educational attainment of best tutoring practices occurred at the "two sigma" level - when compared to standard classroom instruction. This means that if you measure (by testing) the normal range of variation in student attainment after standard classroom lecture presentations, a group of similar tutored students display, on average, educational attainment two standard deviations above the average of the other class. Calling the standard deviation by its statistical name "sigma," we get the challenge expressed as the "two sigma problem." That is, how can you offer group instruction in school such that average class performance is two standard deviations above the mean for ordinary lecture presentations? No other research into educational practices ever demonstrated an "effect size" so large. **I suggest that, without realizing it, Bloom was asking how to get tacit integrations reliably occurring in a classroom setting.**

The next graph displays two curves side by side. The first curve displays the results of testing a class of students using the usual series of lectures and recitations, followed by a summative test to judge how well the class has done in learning the material. The second curve next to it displays the measured effect from a second group of learners who had the advantage of individual tutoring. The difference between the two results is two standard deviations. These graphs are not displaying actual results of the research conducted by Bloom, rather they are showing the effect of his results illustrated in a standard normal curve to make the results easier to see. Some students in the regular class achieved results as good as others in the tutoring group. Bloom explained these results as indicative of superior performance found among the brightest students regardless of how they were taught.

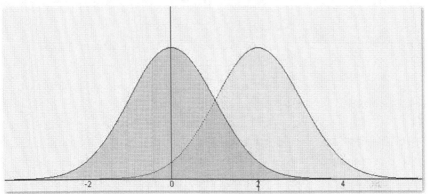

How do you teach the second class so that testing performance is two standard deviations above the mean of the first class?

Bloom supervised a few doctoral dissertations that ran experiments comparing regular classroom instruction to those employing mastery learning techniques and another using one-on-one tutoring. **Mastery learning** removes the effect of the clock. Instruction continues for each student until success is demonstrated at a predetermined level of accomplishment. Only then does the student move forward into new material. Mastery learning offers a one-sigma improvement over regular classroom instruction, but the tutoring process consistently beat even mastery learning. Bloom began a systematic search for other educational factors to add onto mastery learning with the intention of bringing those students up to the level of students who experienced individual tutoring. As of the time of his published results (back in 1984) he found that no combination of instructional strategies were as successful as tutoring. I am making a leap when I assume that an important difference between classroom instruction and tutoring is the greater likelihood of students achieving tacit integrations, hence exhibiting higher comprehension (as when enjoying the Gurr type of assistance with learning). Bloom did find that about 20% of classroom students developed similar mastery of the content as compared to the tutored group, but he identified those students as exceptional. The problem lies with the 80% who could not reach tutored levels of understanding in regular classroom instructional presentations.

The most important single factor uncovered by the various experiments led by Bloom was the presence of a **feedback loop**. Teachers tended to pay more attention to the best students and received little feedback from the weaker members of the class. This practice is consistent with Gurr's steps where he emphasized the need for the student to do the talking in order for the teacher to understand the "disconnects" and the interfering misconceptions. All of these studies reinforce the need for personal attention in helping students achieve tacit integrations; it takes a skilled teacher to provide that kind of attention in a setting with many students in the classroom.

Achievement through use of mastery learning averaged about one standard deviation above the mean compared to regular classroom instruction, a result attributable to the addition of "formative" testing into the mix. These special quizzes provided regular diagnostic information to the teacher who then aimed special help of the right kind to specific students depending on what kinds of difficulties the tests revealed. Mastery learning requires fine-tuning of content offerings to each student and demands a great deal of extra time on the part of the teacher and there's the rub! Automating some of this needed hand-holding offers some hope for the future and can possibly reduce the cost of education.

Technology to the rescue

The two-sigma problem is referenced online by a fascinating site offering (for the moment) free college courses from some of the highest prestige universities on the planet. The organization is called Coursera (https://coursera.org) and is supported by grants. The organization has a thirst for capturing information about how online students function. A significant database on misconceptions and other types of learning interference is being compiled. Their training utilizes some of the most important features found by Bloom and other educational researchers for optimizing education. Knowledge transmission (via video lectures) is offered in short segments and run at the will of the student. Included with these lectures are interactive questions that serve to keep the students on their toes but also offer reinforcement for learning as well as diagnostic information. Coursera captures student answers to these questions for later study, thus uncovering typical confusions found among the student body. With that collected information Coursera can modify the instructional material, offer ways to adjust the typical misconceptions found, and thereby strengthen student engagement. Immediate feedback and repetitious formative testing leads to what Bloom called mastery learning. In addition to Coursera some schools are experimenting with online video lectures offered through the Khan Academy (www.Khanacademy.org), an online community offering free classes for students all over the globe. By "outsourcing" lecture material that use online videos, teachers in regular classrooms can spend more time coaching and less time telling. Some teachers disparage this semi-automation of the teaching process claiming it "corporatizes" education threatening to place profits ahead of learning. I hope both sides of this issue can examine the results with an open mind and come to terms with these new approaches.

With the structure of tacit knowledge pointing to the value of regular feedback (in both directions, to and from the student), any teaching and learning approach that factors in a feedback loop is likely to offer advantages over those that do not. Bloom wished for a way to accomplish this for large class sizes but did not have the technology. Today we have several techniques at hand. Imagine every student in a classroom holding some type of keyboard or device similar to an iPad. The instructor asks a question and can see at a glance on a central computer monitor the various responses of each member of the class. Some students indicate they understand while others are slow to respond, still others offer an incorrect answer. Now the instructor has some idea what types of help will be most helpful to those in the classroom (eSystems, 2013).

Other technologies offer the chance for constructing computerized expert systems interacting one-on-one with individual students. This trend toward sophisticated experimentation into feedback loops is now showing success through computerized "Adaptive Learning" strategies. Companies like Newton (www.knewton.com) and Area9 (area9learning.com) are using powerful computers to analyze student stumbling blocks to learning and can offer automatic special pathways through the instructional materials to show the student how to go beyond misconceptions and provide extra help with missing subsidiary particulars. As the special one-on-one effect of a tutor is becoming computerized, we may expect a revolution coming in the delivery of education. The older teaching machines and programmed instruction were not operating from computerized platforms having as much power as are available today. Critics will worry about machines taking over from live teachers, but teachers exercising proper care and monitoring of these automated classes may yet solve the two-sigma problem. I am encouraged by these developments. Keep in mind some types of classes are not well suited to these advanced computerized instructional systems. Do you want your brain surgeon trained in this manner?

Since the emphasis here is on tacit integrations, hence superior levels of comprehension, we need to examine how the presence of higher orders of understanding is measured. Getting to the next clue requires us to digress for a moment and recall Blooms famous taxonomy but reviewing that taxonomy through the lens of tacit knowledge.

Blooms Taxonomy

It was back in 1954 when the same Benjamin Bloom and his team published the *Taxonomy of Educational Objectives* based on several years of conferences where "college examiners" struggled to organize a way to view the cognitive behavior of students. On page one we read that:

> For example, some teachers believe their students should really understand, others desire their students to internalize knowledge, still others want their students to "grasp the core or essence" or "comprehend." Do they all mean the same thing? Specifically what does a student do who "really understands" which he does not do when he does not understand (Bloom, 1954)

As you can see this Blooms team was thinking about the same sorts of cognitive behavior Polanyi addressed. The taxonomy was developed to make communication easier among educators trying to understand what was meant by "understanding" and specifically how to test for that understanding. Bear in mind that Blooms taxonomy was developed for educational testers and did not intend to be a comprehensive description of all forms of cognitive behavior as demonstrated among seasoned practitioners.

The outcome was a six level categorization of mental behavior; let us briefly review these levels in the light of tacit knowledge.

Level 1 Knowledge. The recall of specific details - like facts, terminology, methodologies, and even theories, - constitutes this first level. Information is essentially memorized and can be recalled or recognized, but is not expected to be actively employed in any creative manner. This kind of knowledge is communicatable in symbolic form therefore is not tacit in structure. Blooms book offers example test questions that are used to assess students' possession of this lowest knowledge level; these tests are simple multiple choice. There are circumstances where a student with a deep tacit knowledge of, say, the behavior of gasses, may answer some particular test questions through their understanding of the phenomenon involved, but the questions can easily be answered from a memorized recall of the relevant fact.

Using our content example of Archimedes' principle, we may ask knowledge based questions with something like this:

You can measure the buoyant force on a floating block of wood by: a) measuring the force needed to push the block under water, b) measuring the volume of the block, or c) measuring the weight of the water displaced by the block. Answer "c" is correct but can be recalled without understanding.

Level 2 Comprehension. This term sounds like we are testing for understanding but the category judges a more limited form of performance. Students are expected to be able to extract meaning from information offered to them in a symbolic form, such as in a written or verbal paragraph. Students take a phrase and then restate it in different words or extrapolate a trend. Test examples illustrate that memorized information is capable of answering many of these questions, however, depending on prior knowledge, the task may be operating at higher cognitive functioning. No clear evidence of tacit knowledge is yet necessary at this level.

A comprehension type question may ask for a definition of Archimedes principal restated using different words.

Level 3 Application. You might understand something well enough to describe it but to apply that understanding to solve a problem containing a novel twist demands higher level capability. No longer will a simple form of memorized knowledge suffice. Possessing tacit knowledge is useful in completing a requested test behavior in this category. When constructing test questions based on application, students receiving the question typically complain that the question is "not fair" because they have not confronted precisely that question as part of the course instruction.

An application question involving Archimedes principle might present the dimensions of a block of wood floating on water, indicate the measured distance of the height of the block above the water surface, and then ask what would happen (quantitatively) if a cylindrical hole of a specified radius were drilled partially into the upper surface of the block of wood. To solve the problem all necessary numerical quantities must be offered to the student except the density of the wood (that is part of the problem). Students must really understand Archimedes' principle to solve such a problem; it requires creativity and ingenuity and some students will not be able to do so. Incidentally, there is a prejudice among educators regarding the use of multiple-choice questions. They seem too simple for measuring more advanced thought processes. I know from experience that a careful test writer can check for application using the right sets of distracters (choices that are wrong because of a subtle failure in logic or knowledge). Answering this type of question generally requires some form of tacit understanding.

Level 4 Analysis. The constituent parts of a complex concept are detected and their interactions figured out and explained. As Bloom says:

"…the ability to distinguish fact from hypothesis in a communication, to identify conclusions and supporting statements, to distinguish relevant from extraneous material, to note how one idea relates to another, to see what unstated assumptions are involved in what is said…etc." [Bloom, 1954. p.144]

Analysis takes comprehension to a higher level where the meaning of a complex idea is dissected. Note that as we work upwards through the taxonomy, cognitive requirements become more stringent and a full tacit knowledge of the content more helpful - yet not necessarily always required. Notice also that measurable educational outcomes are always in mind within Blooms Taxonomy, hence the references to "communication" as in "something written" presented in a testing format. How well the students respond to tests that grow in complexity as we work to ever-higher levels of the taxonomy is being judged and categorized. At this stage, although tests center on specific content, there is an underlying understanding on the part of the student that thinking behaviors such as judging hypotheses and assessing the strength of assertions are presumed to be known and understood. What may be called "critical thinking" is under evaluation rather than just a higher level of knowledge about some complex topic. Polanyi made a distinction between analytical thought of a tightly focused kind and the operation of a deeper tacit appreciation of the subject

matter. For example, we may ask a student to design and analyze an experiment showing how Archimedes' principle explains the operation of raising and lowering a submarine. The Cartesian diver device (shown here) is an apparatus applicable to this problem and could be made available to help the student accomplish this task. Do students themselves think about Blooms levels of knowledge? Regrettably, I have seen little evidence of that in my career as professor and often reflect upon a need to address this deficit in formal education.

Level 5 Synthesis. Students pull together parts of a dimly perceived whole and construct a new pattern not clearly seen. Creativity is put into play as a new "whole" not previously fully explicated is developed. Does this behavior require tacit integrations? Within the scope of the taxonomy the intent is for the student to build upon some newly offered material and previously studied content, such that a new holistic perception is recognized and can be communicated. Polanyi talked about how tacit knowledge leads to a kind of foresight through which an explanatory structure is hinted at from a sense of the subsidiary particulars, but before a full tacit integration occurs. This feature underlies the discovery process that, in the case of science, takes the form of a hidden hypothesis slowly evolving into consciousness. Searching for an example outside the scientific realm, consider the task of a theater director who must confront the specifics of a script and envision how a set design, costumes, actors, and a mood established by lighting all converge to create a complete unified whole realized in a stage production. All the elements that comprise this production are synthesized in a manner that is appreciated by the audience. The synthesis category does not anticipate the full execution of whatever is being synthesized; rather, it refers to visualizing and preparing a plan allowing for later execution. In addition, the design of a house constitutes an example of synthesis, as does an exercise in creative writing. Cognitive behaviors outlined in all previous categories are likely to show up here - pulled together in a unified manner. Archimedes came upon his principle when confronted with a problem. When shown a crown that looked like gold, how could you determine that it really was gold without cutting off a piece, hence damaging it? If the teacher or text has not explained this problem, students could be asked to pull together (synthesize) all the comprehension they have gained about the principle to plan a series of actions and measurements leading to a definitive statement about what the crown is made of. Tacit knowledge is surely required here.

Most tellingly and impressively Bloom and his community of thirty two experts anticipated Polanyian structure within the synthesis section of their book by discussing focal consciousness, its alternative, the peripheral, and the creative act of integrating the two. They regarded integration as a creative act. They recognized but disagreed with many thinkers who downgraded the creativity of the synthesis process if the outcome fails to offer new knowledge. I am continually amazed at the richness of thought to be found in this old Bloom book and am pleased to see it still used in teacher training programs today. When critics of education dismiss teacher training in the area of pedagogy, they only display ignorance regarding the huge and valuable amount of knowledge gained over a hundred years regarding how we learn and the resulting best teaching practices.

Level 6 Evaluation. Criteria of value are used to judge the effectiveness of a complex entity. Mere casual opinions are viewed as lacking in careful thought; therefore, the value category passes over snap judgments as insufficiently grounded in the careful consideration needed to properly judge and develop a full evaluation. Only someone with a deep and expert understanding of the relevant content is considered able to make defendable, evaluative judgments. This category level may seem less advanced than the effort of synthesis, and Bloom recognizes the problem but insists that adding into the cognitive mix a sense of valuation raises the bar on mental effort. Judgments of the value of an effort require application of internal and external standards and criteria. For example, as a plan is executed for creating a theatrical production, evaluation is continually being employed, thus causing changes to be made as the process continues. A creative writer is evaluating content and style when revising and improving the product. Perhaps asking a student to evaluate a test on Archimedes' principle offers an example of behavior at this sixth level.

Although not explicitly defined, Blooms committee hints of a final mental capability level beyond category six that addresses the production of new knowledge as the final pinnacle of cognitive attainment. Blooms committee then sensed an insight they hoped to be elucidated in the future when they briefly mentioned consciousness:

> "If the level of consciousness can be demonstrated to be an important dimension in the classification of behavior, it would pose a great range of problems and point to a whole new set of relationships which would be of interest to researchers in the field of educational psychology. One might hope that it would provide a basis for explaining why behaviors which are initially displayed with a high degree of consciousness *become, after some time and repetition, automatic or are accompanied by a low level of consciousness.*" [Bloom, 1954, p.20]

I highlighted a phrase above indicating these educators anticipated the insights of Polanyi without knowing what he said about tacit knowledge! Recent research into educational psychology is now integrated into a valuable new book updating the original Bloom Taxonomy and is well worth a visit (Anderson, et al., 2002)

Constructivism

Of the many "isms" in the field of educational psychology one of the most relevant is inadvertently founded upon the theory of tacit knowledge and is called *Human Constructivism*. A basic tenet of this view of learning and teaching is that knowledge is not a rigid structure of information imparted directly into the brains of students by teachers, but instead teachers offer a service that guides learners toward internal construction of the understandings desired. Constructivists, deemphasize rote learning, typically indicated by the presence of long lectures, cookbook laboratory exercises, passive video watching, problem solving using fill-in-the-blank formulas, and some versions of repetitive drill. Professionals see learning instead as a process somewhat similar to the discovery of new knowledge. Experts pull together the results of experiments and experiences and incorporate prior understandings to construct new breakthroughs. Students ideally exhibit the same behaviors with the advantage of a teacher guide along with recommended techniques that help in the learning process. There are plenty of skeptics warning against the constructivist cause; their voices are offered here shortly.

Constructivists offer a number of tools for helping students through the process of "constructing" their comprehension. In the discipline of science I refer, for example, to the book *Teaching Science for Understanding* (Wandersee & Novak, 2005), and *Elementary Science Methods* (Martin, 2012). Key techniques of constructivism include directing attention to pre-existing ideas (possibly incorrect) held by the student, followed by offering experiences designed to challenge the prior knowledge. Through experiments and activities the learners **construct** new ways of understanding and overcome prior misconceptions. The structure

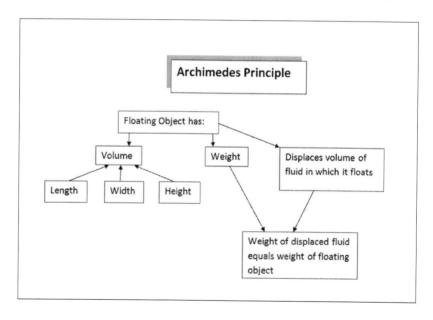

of the knowledge is often imagined as collections of facts and information built into a pattern called a *schema* by Jean Piaget. He is recognized as a leading predecessor to constructivist thinking. Although buried in the mind, schema is crudely represented on paper by explicit collections of ideas and facts organized within sets of balloon shapes. The facts and ideas are related to one another. The relationships are shown by drawing connecting lines linking the relevant ideas together.

These drawings are called **concept maps** that organize explicitly the implicit particulars into a visual pattern of linked facts and ideas and at differing levels of detail. We will have more to say about constructivism in part V.

This simplified example of a concept map offers an explicit listing of the various particulars needed to grasp Archimedes' Principle but the presence of the symbolic content in the boxes, although possibly embedded within the mind of the learner, **is not**

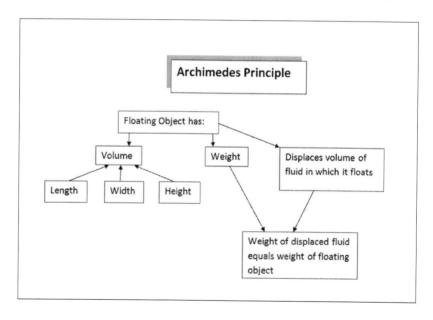

necessarily in the form of subsidiary awareness. The concept map is thus a tool, but not an end in itself, as it represents particulars on their way toward forming the needed tacit integration.

The preceding pages offer a sampling of a few highlights from educational psychology and nothing to suggest Polanyi was wrong has yet surfaced. Now we need to look directly at the gears turning inside the brain.

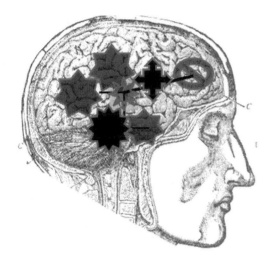

What have cognitive psychologists learned about how the mind works that add credibility to our understanding of the structure of tacit knowing? We seek additional practical suggestions for learners and teachers to follow as we build comprehension and search for insight. What about the skeptics who have a hard time dealing with so-called mystical, hidden mental functioning? The detective story continues as we search for clues in more contemporary research.

<u>Chapter Five: Further Research</u>

Michael Polanyi worked out his ideas on tacit knowledge during the late forties and early fifties before most breakthroughs in our understanding of cognitive psychology, brain structure and neuronal functioning took place. Let us continue the detective work as we seek additional clues within contemporary research. We investigate the mind from the viewpoint of scientists who study how the brain is made and how it seems to work. Because a key feature of research is the need to tighten the scope of an experiment to a tiny subset of a subject, you will rarely find broad scale academic studies on something as vague as tacit knowledge. The exception is found in philosophy journals, review articles in the fields of knowledge management (business), and clinical medicine (especially nursing). We will search through these areas as well as review research in artificial intelligence, neuroscience, and wherever else scientists have ventured. As we explore relevant academic research, keep in mind the key operative word remains *insight*. Whenever that contentious word, insight, appears, scholars are referring to a mysterious moment when somehow an elusive failure to understand something suddenly morphs through a flash into a state of comprehension. This is recognized and accepted as the "Aha!" moment. I have not found anyone denying the existence of this effect.

Considerable confusion arises out of attempts to explain it and I am pleased to report that serious experimental and theoretical work is underway at last to understand what Polanyi knew as tacit integration.

Cognitive Psychology

Psychologists have a long history of avoiding consciousness and insight. These topics were long considered too vague to be tackled in a scientific way; recently, however, a wave of serious research is spreading throughout psychology offering significant results. Psychology is a broad field of study but those who focus on the mind are generally referred to as *cognitive psychologists.* Let us pull together a consensus view of how the field sees and interprets insight. Remember that I am interested in the tacit theory of knowledge, but since psychologists rarely go there, we are forced to begin with the closest place we can get, the nature of insight.

How can you conduct experiments involving insight?

Insight comes with a huge, built-in problem. Insight is too mysterious, too hidden, presumably buried in the subconscious, and that makes the scientific study of insight quite difficult. An example is found from research using problems well known for needing the application of insight. The **Remote Associates Test** (Mednick, 1967) offers that type of problem. Consider the following three words: COIN, QUICK, and SPOON. The task is to find a fourth word, which can be paired with each of the first three to make a sensible two-word phrase. These tests are sufficiently specific and well designed to make the presence of more than that one extra word extremely unlikely. For the three example words above the fourth word is SILVER. Hence we may speak of "silver spoon," "quicksilver,"or "coin silver". Your brain is likely to try generating the answer word through application of conscious trial and error. You try as many words as you can think of as fast as you can. Eventually you might stumble across the target word. Alternatively the subconscious mind works on the problem and suddenly the right word seems to pop into consciousness without effort leading you to feel that special "aha" moment and to wonder where the word came from.

Psychologists use this remote associates test to study the characteristics of insight in a laboratory setting. By clever arrangements of similar trials, they can "prime" the test subjects with the answer in ways that leave the subject unaware of the priming. Under these conditions, insight occurs more often and faster, hence indicating that *unconscious processing is taking place*. Curiously the test is a somewhat backwards tacit integration. The combination of each of the three words with the target word yields three entirely different focal wholes to which each test word serves as a subsidiary particular. For example, silver spoon, quick silver and coin silver are three wildly different concepts that are related only using the target word silver. The experiment is asking for that one word which serves simultaneously as a subsidiary particular for three different wholes to which they contribute. The point I am making is that scientists are now cleverly studying the structure of tacit integration without explicitly referring to Polanyi's theory.

Building upon experiments like this one and hundreds of others, the psychologists were the ones to separate insight into those several stages we met earlier. Slightly different versions of these stages are discussed in what seems to be the bible for insight, a book called, *The Nature of Insight* (Sternberg & Davidson, 1995). You should recall *Immersion* (sometimes called *Preparation)*, *Incubation* where elapsed time offers a chance for the material to become processed somehow and reconnected so that *Illumination* strikes thereby offering insight. The meaning of the insight may seem clear to the experiencer yet sometimes-technical details need to be worked during the final stage called *verification*. Polanyi was well versed in these stages but a few details are vague and need clarity. Incubation is troublesome to psychologists because some believe, as does Polanyi, that significant mental activity is occurring beneath consciousness. The nature of the insight itself is also an area of disagreement since the flash of sudden understanding is inherently too magical for comfort. Digging into the heart of these two topics shines a spotlight directly onto tacit integration. More detective work is needed to search necessary clues regarding these concerns.

Incubation

A wide variety of psychological research studies support the existence of these subconscious mental processes and one clue is found in a study on incubation time. The effects of incubation time on problem solving were studied by Ut Na Sio and Ormerod in a meta-analysis that combined statistically the results of 117 incubation research studies. They discovered that, despite a few negative results, incubation time did offer a measurable and positive effect on successful task completion, especially for efforts requiring creative and divergent thinking. For some types of tasks a long preparation time of study associated with conscious effort enhanced the value of incubation - a behavior already encountered here called *immersion*. They also measured the effect of different types of incubation activity and discovered that high cognitive effort taking place during incubation time led to poorer results (Sio & Ormerod, 2009). That finding reinforces the need for incubation time to be a relatively easy and mindless pursuit.

Intuition

Since the topic of intuition has already come up and appears to be confounded with tacit knowing, we need to review the subject using the perspectives offered by cognitive psychologists.

In the published research literature, I have found many different cognitive behaviors identifiable as demonstrating the workings of intuition. We want to look at these and see if tacit knowledge and its integration are detectable therein. We need to employ useful terminology found within the psychological literature - the most relevant being our old friend, schema. Recall that a schema is a mental structure organizing facts and information. When we possess schemata (plural), we may say that we understand complicated things. For example when I understand Archimedes principal, such that problems about floating and sinking are solvable by me, we may say that I have built into my head a schema about floating and sinking which is a mental representation of all the various particulars making up the total picture. A tacit integration may (but not necessarily) result from the schema and, thus, we feel that we understand the complicated thing. Note the word "concept" refers to a relatively simple mental entity; hence, we may need a collection of integrated concepts to compose the entire schema. The idea of volume is a concept, as is also the weight of a certain amount of fluid. Facts link together into a concept that, when combined with other concepts, build a schema. All of these mental parts must make sense together. We use the schema as a representational template for understanding and problem solving. If the schema is constructed in the mind subconsciously rather than as an explicit concept map, the term intuition is applicable when referencing such a schema.

For example, an action schema for **simple harmonic motion** may arise from extensive childhood experience while playing on a swing. What does it *feel* like to play on a swing? Back and forth, back and forth, swing up high and stop for an instant, then fall backwards swooping past the low point on the swing (now at the highest speed) until you stop again at the top (high up on the other side). This behavior is felt in the gut. The dynamic features of oscillatory motion would in this case be "encoded" at a pre-verbal level based only on the feeling. The possessor of the schema is not likely to explain verbally what they know about "simple harmonic motion" yet can use that inarticulate experiential knowledge to answer questions about how the swing behaves. Contrast this intuitive schema with the knowledge about simple harmonic motion coded into the form of an equation. The intuitive person exhibiting a feeling for the behavior of a swing is not likely to recognize the oscillatory behavior represented through an unfamiliar symbolic language (the equation). Several specialists in the field of business management explain this type of intuition as a phenomenon drawing upon tacit knowledge accumulated through experience and retrieved for later use by pattern recognition (Pira, 2011). An experienced guide may help students recognize how the equation expresses what they already know through intuition. The exercise of mapping an intuitive scheme into equation form helps build intuitive knowledge about mathematics.

Srinivasa Ramanujan, a famous mathematician from India, defied all sensible expectations for a poor clerk by filling notebooks with incredible conjectures and mathematical theorems that amazed the world's leading mathematicians. He ended up at Trinity College, Cambridge University, where his prodigious creative inventions earned him membership as a fellow in the Royal Society. Those who knew him puzzled over the nature of his mental gifts.

Some called him a magician since nobody had a clue about how he came up with the insights that later offered them years of intense analytical exploration. Others recognized the mysterious, seemingly unconscious mental processing that would suddenly spring to life, as intuition. One of Ramanujans key mentors, who refused to speculate about mystical internal mental states, did agree that evidence for the unconscious nature of his earth shaking insights was overwhelming (Kanigel, 1991. P. 286.) Ramanujans discoveries appear to be identifiable as intuition at its highest level of expression.

So what is intuition?

The idea is sufficiently vague to have generated more than a few definitions, but the one that seems to have the strongest staying power refers to the making of an inference unconsciously. An explicit (conscious) inference is made when a belief or statement is accepted because it is based analytically upon supporting facts (Beardsley, 1975). If the tacit mind contains a number of linked subsidiary particulars, then it might use these elements to generate an inference - but unconsciously. The resulting inference pops up into consciousness without the mind knowing the exact sequence of logical thought processes that generated the inference. Intuitive inferences are not necessarily correct. Gigerenzer observed that conscious, logical thought processes are sometimes at odds with intuition (Gigerenzer, 2007)

I recall a number of group decision exercises I ran in a corporate environment involving teams of workers tasked with choosing a best course of action. Point values were assigned to the different possibilities, and the solution with the highest score was chosen as the best one. Invariably some members of the team expressed surprise and dismay at the outcome but were not able to articulate the reason for disputing an obviously logical process for selecting the best choice. Their intuition was identifying the logical outcome as suboptimal. Further group discussion resulted in choosing a course of action different from the one developed by the scored exercise. Sometimes explicit exercises are used as tools for teasing out of the tacit realm a hidden preferred choice rather than a consciously derived one. If anything, the theory of tacit knowledge strengthens respect for the operation of intuition since it provides a theoretical framework for how the mind could make an unconscious inference.

Gigerenzer conducted an experiment asking expert golfers and novices to pay explicit attention to details of their swing. The novices performed better than experts did. You should know why. Experts broke subsidiary awareness by applying focal awareness to details of the swing, hence leading to poorer performance (Gigerenzer, 2007, p. 33).

Using the terminology of educational psychology we may say that if a person has an established **schema** for, say, a golf swing, and if the individual particulars making up that schema are tacitly integrated (not always the case), then the behavior of the person appears to follow the principles of tacit knowledge. On the other hand some schemata may be only an explicit collection of relevant facts and concepts existing in the mind as a conscious map instead of a tacit integration. The behavior of the person is then not likely to reflect the presence of tacit knowledge. Therefore, we should be careful to avoid automatically assuming schemata as being coincident with what Polanyi had in mind when he described how we know things in a tacit sense.

I repeatedly find in the educational literature recognition of cognitive behaviors consistent with the structure of tacit knowledge yet without any reference to Polanyi and his thought.

There is a problem with assembling, then pulling together, all the necessary subsidiary particulars needed for comprehending some complex entity. The conscious mental space in the brain available to hold all these parts is limited. This is another rich research area examined by cognitive psychologists and directs us to look for more clues.

Working Memory (includes Short Term Memory)

Computer models of learning are used to mimic how the brain works. Some studies examine the use of working memory in the capture of particulars needed for eventual integration (Polanyi's perspective). To grasp the entirety of a complex idea requires gathering and putting all the particulars leading up to that idea into a working memory "space" within the brain. Experiments have shown that our short-term memory size permits only a limited amount of particulars: estimated as containing only 4 to 7 bits of information. At the beginning of a learning attempt, we fruitlessly try to jam too much stuff into temporary memory and find that it just does not fit. An interesting example of working memory limitation hit me recently while reading a fascinating book on the brain called *Brain Bugs* (Buonomano, 2012). The following discussion digs into working memory but asks for some serious effort on your part, the reader. Use your own discretion on how much energy to invest in the next several pages.

What is in it for me?

I do believe this is a high point of the book because we get to examine in detail the process of gaining comprehension of something that, while difficult, does not require a considerable amount of prerequisite knowledge. You do not need higher level mathematics but must be willing to take some time to think carefully.

Illustrating Development of Comprehension: *The Monty Hall Problem*

Buonomano describes a well-known problem that gives a perspective on the intuitive understandings that we humans fail to acquire regarding basic probability theory. This example is called *The Monty Hall Problem*. I will describe it too you with the warning that, as I write this, I have failed to understand it myself - despite a considerable background in statistics, including teaching the subject in college and corporate settings. The attempt to understand this problem includes an example of working memory limitations and points to the need for juggling many explicit facts all at the same time. Follow along as we try to make sense of this puzzle together.

Do you remember the TV show *Lets Make a Deal* hosted by Monty Hall? Contestants were shown three doors. Behind one of them hid a valuable prize while behind the other two stood a waiting goat, a symbol of failure for those who did not pick the prize. A reader of *Parade* magazine mailed in a question to the very smart columnist Marilyn vos Savant asking for help about a hypothetical probability puzzle based on a variation of this show.

Suppose when confronted with the three doors as described before (A, B, and C) you chose one of them (let us say you picked C). Before going further with the exercise, think about the probability that you will win the prize. By the way, because you are being asked to think about a math problem, does this question stir up some internal emotions of stress because you are being asked to think about a math problem? If so, you suffer from math anxiety that interferes with the size of working memory. Teachers need to be aware that many of us have this problem. Under these circumstances, it helps to just stop for a moment, recognize your stress, try to set aside the worry, and then go on where you left off. At least you are reading this book privately and need not answer me aloud! That is a relief!

What is the probability that you will pick the correct door? To answer this question, start with the number of different ways there are to pick the right door. The answer is one. There is only one prize behind one door. How many ways in all can I pick any door? There are three doors so the answer is three. Divide one by three and you get the probability that you will choose the right door (one chance out of three). The probability is one third. Does the probability calculation make no sense to you? You might tell the teacher you are stuck (hence exposing yourself to a class of students some of whom might be silently jeering at you for being so dumb). That concern stops many students from raising their hand but now let us say you are brave and really want to understand this so you raise your hand. The teacher or tutor can help by offering another example. Say you are on a team and need to flip a coin to see which side begins a game. If a "head" pops up you win and your team starts the game. What is the probability that you will get heads? First count the total number of all different ways the coin can come up. There are two sides to the coin so the answer is two. Now how many ways can you get a head? Only one head exists so there is only one way to get it. Divide the number of ways you win by all the ways a coin can come up. One divided by two is one-half, or fifty/fifty, or a probability of winning of fifty percent. This sidebar illustrates the critical importance of feedback in learning (by the way, a sophisticated computer program can discover you are confused by checking your answers to a series of questions and then programmatically offer the right intervention to help move you forward).

Go back to the Monty Hall problem. Save some of your short-term memory by writing the probability of guessing the correct door on a piece of paper so it is easy to recall. Alternatively you are invited to try to remember the answer, one third, and stick it into short-term memory just to challenge yourself in continuing with this problem.

Here comes the trick. Suppose Monty Hall (knowing your choice – its C, remember?) now opens one of the *other* doors (one that you did not pick, say door B) behind which is found a goat. Then he says to you that with the *new* information provided, *do you wish to change your answer - pick a different door*? My immediate judgment is that now I have a new, higher probability to win (one-half) and see no reason why either door A or door C could offer a better chance of winning. Therefore, I decide not to bother changing my answer. The smart journalist disagrees and insists that I should change my guess. This paradox **is** the Monty Hall problem. How can switching your guess now be better?

Incidentally, at this moment, right now, while I write this sentence, I forget which door I picked. I must go back and look it up (oh yes, it was C), a symptom of limits to working memory. However, I do not understand why it is better for me to change my answer (from C to A). So what does author Buonomano say about switching the answer? Well, he first notes that the probability of getting the wrong answer at the very beginning of the game is 2/3 (that is there are two ways of being wrong out of three choices). Suppose the prize is really behind door A but we have chosen C, we will get it wrong. Then he points out that 2/3 of the time switching answers will get it right. But wait! How can changing the first guess be more right? There is a blockage to understanding here and I do not know what is causing that blockage. Perhaps part of my problem is *fixation*. The theory of tacit knowledge warns us that we get off track with misconceptions, missing subsidiary elements, or fixation on the wrong idea. Since there is nothing extra added to the explanation, and I am stuck, I might be focused on the *wrong thing*. Remember this example is offered in the context of trying to create a tacit integration of all the subsidiary particulars (hence understanding the problem) and highlights the need for holding a lot of stuff in working memory. When first trying to understand a complex idea we must get all the particulars into the mind and the starting point is use of working memory. We begin with explicit facts but in order to understand something complex, all the details of that thing must be held in the mind all at the same time and accessible in a subsidiary form of awareness. The advantage of using tacit knowledge is that with enough practice (repetition of the elements of the problem) we gradually get those facts and concepts rooted as subsidiary particulars into long-term memory. These particulars become programmed into automated neuron links of activation so that we are not relying upon conscious, working memory to hold everything. The subsidiary awareness does it for us. However, the conscious struggle needed to understand a problem requires that all the stuff needed to understand the problem must first be placed explicitly into working memory. How do you do that? Often too much stuff must fit without enough mental space to fit it. Getting the details rewired later into the form of subsidiary particulars takes time (and is called practice). In addition, the self-conscious worry about being perceived as "dumb" chews up additional, valuable space in short term memory along with generating a negative feeling state. All of this leads to anxiety. No wonder so many students turn away from math and science or any other hard subject.

Short-term memory is helped by "chunking." This means that multiple pieces of fact or bits of understandings need to be bundled together. In his famous research paper of 1954, George Miller described the limits of short-term memory using a phrase "The Magical Number seven plus or minus two..." He discovered that minds typically store only that many bits of information for short periods. If additional information is linked through meaningful association, more bits can be stored such as the format of a telephone number that has ten digits. Chunking is a technique for increasing the amount of information that is held in short term memory. New research suggests we are limited to only 4 bits of information.

When examining the Monty Hall problem, you need to hold in memory, at the same time, the 1/3 probability of choosing the *right* door, the apparent fifty/fifty chance of picking the right door *after* a goat is revealed, along with the 2/3 chance of picking the *wrong* door before the goat is revealed AND that switching doors results in a 2/3 chance of getting it right (don't understand that yet). Reviewing these items repeatedly can chunk the information together and automate them as subsidiary particulars ready for integration thus bringing about the "Aha!" relief of understanding. Chunking by converting bits of information into subsidiary particulars usually occurs during incubation time when you are doing something else like running a sweeper.

By the way, Aha has not happened to me yet with respect to this Monty Hall problem. I have not yelled, "Got it" (my long-suffering wife could point out that some more lawn mowing is in order). Let us go back to the claimed probability of getting the guess wrong 2/3 of the time. If the likelihood of the first guess being wrong is 2/3 then does switching answers increase the probability of getting it right? Somehow, I get a glimmer of "vaguely possible" but I still do not feel comfortable about it. Buonomano goes on to say that switching answers means the probability of getting it right becomes 2/3 of the time. Hey, that was the probability of getting it wrong in the first place! This is just crazy!

OK, it is time to give this problem a rest. Go away. Do something else for a while. Throw another log on the fire and cut some more firewood, *Its incubation time!*

Welcome me back everyone! A few days have elapsed (avoiding further writing) and I can report that I now understand the answer to this problem! In order for understanding to take place I needed to see all the subsidiary particulars in just the right manner and *all at once*. Since I did not have a teacher to ask, I tried Google and found a great explanation on Wikipedia (The Monty Hall problem). Sometimes getting just the right explanation is what we need and sometimes folks need different types of explanations.

Since working memory has such limitations, Wikipedia constructed a "decision table" that allows us to see all the ways this game show can play out and then we can determine probabilities of different outcomes. The table frees us from having all this stuff jammed into working memory all at once. This illustrates for us that organization of the required information is highly important and is one of the things that you can do to help yourself. Immersion in all the facts and relationships can help bring about the right organization to allow the breakthrough.

Behind Door C	Behind Door A	Behind Door B	Result if Keeping the Guess	Result if Switching the Guess
Prize	Goat	Goat	*Prize*	Goat
Goat	Prize	Goat	Goat	*Prize*
Goat	Goat	Prize	Goat	*Prize*

Look at the table. We started out the Monty Hall game by choosing door C and the table displays the various ways this choice can play out. If the prize is really behind door C (first row in the table above) then we were right to choose it and would be wrong if we switched our choice to either A or B (depending on where the revealed goat happens to be). However if a goat is really behind door C, then keeping that choice is wrong and for **two different instances of the goat being behind door C** (second row and the third row in the table) hence switching the guess yields the prize under two different conditions instead of just one! Switching the answer raises the probability of getting the prize to 2/3 from 1/3. The reason for this curious result is that Monty Hall is *forced* to reveal the location of a goat *after* our first guess is publically revealed hence we have more information than we did before and switching the guess increases the probability of success. Monty is *forced* to reveal only a door that has a goat behind it. The probability calculations are based on *all three ways* this game plays out. That is a key point! If you only examine one case of these three ways you do not get the entire picture. Statisticians call filling out all the outcomes the *sample space*. By focusing attention on only one of the three ways the problem can occur, we fail to recognize the impact of the two other possibilities.

I was not able to grasp the book explanation entirely using my limited working memory nor was I breaking out of the single case mind set. Seeing the answer relied upon looking at a constructed table displaying all three cases, then, by examining the table, I could see how all the different possibilities affect the total probability calculation. After going through the table analysis, I finally *believe* in the answer described in Buonomano's book. Test this claim for yourself. Play around with the various "what if" scenarios (suppose you chose door B first – what happens….) and see if you are also convinced that the unintuitive claim is true. For me the moment of recognition was more like a bit of fog lifting than an eruption of "Aha!" The tacit theory of knowledge does not always require an instantaneous integration. Sometimes the merging of all the particulars takes place slowly. The feeling of belief, of conviction, however, is critical.

Before we rejoice too quickly, there is the possibility for lingering doubt in your mind. Probabilities usually change when the amount of information changes, which is why the immediate intuitive analysis suggests that with only two doors to choose from the probability, must now be fifty/fifty. Now I am reminded of that picture of two women; you see one of them or the other but not both at the same time. The danger is that you can seemingly understand the official, consensus analysis of this paradox (switch the answer) but then can shift your integration to the other competing fifty/fifty analysis. Both cannot really be true at the same time. One view is correct and the other is wrong. Remember that your first choice takes place under the conditions of three unknown doors. Check out the online simulation of the Monty hall problem on the New York Times website:

[http://www.nytimes.com/2008/04/08/science/08monty.html?_r=1&],

Here you see how the problem looks from *behind* the doors (Monty's view). Run the simulator and watch many "runs" of the game. See how the results of many trials prove the contestant has two ways of winning when switching.

But wait again! The game is not played a number of times. It is played ONCE! So how do we interpret the outcome of many trials? The multiplicity of trials just serves to measure, in real time, the actual probabilities for doing the game repeatedly. So although you play the real game (on TV) *once*, are the chances of winning still better if you switch? The skeptical mind can flip again the coherent integration back to the fifty/fifty solution. Two doors make the choice fifty/fifty and not 2/3rds so how is switching better? After all, when offered the opportunity to switch, you are facing two doors and not three. Unless your first choice is the prize, one of the switched doors is certainly the prize (Monty is not allowed by the rules to reveal the prize) and the other is, of course, just the other goat. We have a tacit integration problem here just like the drawing of the old lady (seen one way) or the young lady seen the other way. So which is correct? We already know that computer simulations show that switching is better but how can we shut down the wrong image? I found another way to look at the problem on a wonderful intuitive-based math website (Azad, 2013). Change the protocol of the game show very slightly. Ask the contestant to think about the other two doors not chosen. Switching your choice is really like choosing *both* of the other doors. Monty could say that if you switch he will let you chose *both* doors even though at least one of them must be a goat. Whichever one is the prize will be considered as your choice. The door that is the goat will be shown to you as a matter of curiosity. It is a curious argument but, in effect, when you switch, you get to switch to *two doors at once.* Monty Hall leaves the good one for you possibly to win while revealing the bad one. He actually opens the goat door before you make the switch but the effect is still the same, you get to pick two doors instead of one. So switching offers a 2/3 probability of getting the prize.

Where does tacit knowledge come into play here? A tacit integration of the many subsidiary particulars involved in this paradoxical problem must occur in order for you to *feel* that you get it. This is a feeling of "belief." I can believe a thing to be true if the subsidiary particulars are consistent and if they hang together. Buonomano's explanation did not work for me and neither did the various explanations listed in the Wikipedia site. My own analysis of the table of sample spaces did help me as well as the simulation offered by the New York Times and I *really* believed in the answer after seeing the explanation offered on Azad's site. It all came together and I could "see" how it works. Amazingly, our minds recognize when something is understood or is not understood.

Education faces a powerful challenge. A learner must be seriously involved in the learning process. The sense that you understand the Monty Hall problem can only result from a great deal of serious attention paid to the problem. A lazy person (who does not care) may claim they understand something when in actuality they do not. This behavior presents a challenge to the teacher. Unless learners are serious and intent on doing the learning, comprehension will not likely take place. Achievement of comprehension is a creative act of personal insight and is accompanied by a feeling of belief in the answer. **When looked at in this manner, we recognize tacit knowledge as an active mental** *process* **rather than as a categorical** *type* **of knowledge.**

Before putting old Monty to bed, do consider that within the context of this book, there is no requirement to "get it." No test is lurking on the horizon, you will get no course grade, and hence, you may simply accept the strangeness of the paradox as an example of the need for forming a tacit integration. Either push further into the problem as a challenge to test the actions needed by you to finally understand, or choose to pass this by as you continue on the detective journey looking for more clues as we seek to understand more about tacit knowledge. The Azad website is an active demonstration of how to explain things in a manner designed to best activate a deep and more intuitive understanding. If you want to learn some topics in mathematics, you cannot go wrong beginning with that site.

The latest evidence for a tacit cognitive system was just published at the time of the writing of this book. Psychologists argue about the possible existence of multiple mental structures for learning and thinking. Lead researcher J. David Smith at the

University of Buffalo along with several colleagues, conducted an experiment they claim provides the strongest evidence so far in showing that brains have more than one cognitive system. This study is consistent with claims that declarative (explicit) and procedural (tacit) mental processes are different.

The experiment consisted of blocked feedback learning which prevented the use of tacit knowledge development. Learning took place in a declarative, explicit manner. In effect, they "unplugged" the **implicit** learning system in the brain and left the other system intact and working. They concluded that the explicit-conscious and the implicit-procedural systems are different processes in the brain (Smith, Zakrzewski, Roeder, Church, & Ashby, 2013)

Neuroscience is now popular among those who are curious about the functioning of the mind, so we must of course, take a quick peek at discoveries in that arena.

Neuroscience

A huge, growing and recent arena for current research aims to uncover the deepest level of explanation for how the brain functions. The brain is built out of individual cells called neurons. By comparison, houses are constructed from joists, studs, and rafters while the brain is built from a structure of interconnected neurons. These cells come in a variety of special types but in general, we find inside the neuronal cell a nucleus, a relatively long "tail" called the axon (along which an electrical signal travels) and a series of shorter tendrils called dendrites that allow electrical conduction to other neurons. Scientists estimate that over a hundred trillion connections exist in the brain between the 86 billion or so neurons; and the outcome is both **conscious and unconscious activity within the mind** (Buonomano, 2012). You can imagine that figuring out what all these connections do is a herculean task not yet finished (perhaps never to be finished). Do these recent sophisticated discoveries hint at the existence of tacit knowledge?

Most of what happens in the brain takes place below conscious awareness. Perhaps only 5% of brain function supports conscious activity while the other 95% passes by without our knowing about it. Is this where the famous claim comes from that we only use 10% of our brain? This claim is misleading because the entire brain is very busy - even if you are not able to direct your conscious attention to all that is happening. In fact, if you needed to be conscious of everything the brain is doing each nanosecond, you are likely to go insane from the complexity overload! Leonard Mlodinow measured the energy requirement of a brain playing a chess game to a brain simply "spacing out" (meditating) and found that only an extra 1% of energy is needed for that focused, conscious brain to keep up with chess moves (Mlodinow, 2012).

So what is the 95% doing? Some of it monitors all the autonomic functions of bodily parts, such as breathing and maintaining balance as we stand waiting for the bus to show up. Other parts consist of what a computer programmer might call subroutines that trigger when a need arises for their specialized activities. Since they occur without consciousness, Christof Koch calls these subroutines **"zombie agents"** (Koch, 2012).

Some zombie agents control simple reflexes, such as the blink of an eye when a burst of air strikes it, but the more interesting ones develop from experience; these learned zombie programs are highly complex linkages between thousands of neurons caused by the firing of synapses. The structure builds from training through repetition and reinforcement. Resulting zombie agents become a complex sequence of actions that accomplish a skillful act. The assembly of neuronal firings in a zombie subroutine develops from considerable practice (exemplified by muscle memory on the part of athletes). In this manner, we bring about a long-term shift away from attention-hogging conscious processing to automatic and unconscious behavior. I was struck by Koch's observation that if the skilled performer shifts attention to a small subset of the automated task, the skilled action is derailed (recall my earlier example of the failed golf swings due to conscious directed attention to details of the swing). I described this effect earlier as a critical component to tacit knowing. Focal attention paid to a subsidiary particular breaks awareness of the coherent tacit whole. This neurological finding is a significant clue. Apparently, elements we have described as comprising the theory of tacit knowledge exist within a context of current research into the behavior of neurons. Let us look further for more of these confirming discoveries.

Research is finding neurological correlates to subsidiary particulars and tacit integrations operating within the brain.

Koch claims there is a difference between attention and consciousness. Since the tacit theory of knowledge centers around the way we are focally aware vs. the **subsidiary awareness of individual particulars**, this issue of awareness, attention, and consciousness, bears careful examination. Koch makes the point that internal mechanisms directing attention are *separate from* consciousness. Experiments have demonstrated the amazing ability of the attention zombie to aim the spotlight of attention onto some small aspect of sensory input *without consciousness even being directly involved*. The brain reacts to that input while the conscious mind remains focused elsewhere. Polanyi made much of focal vs. subsidiary awareness without the benefit of most current research into modern neuroscience. He claimed that subsidiary awareness ranges over the full spectrum of vague consciousness to full unconsciousness. Current discoveries in neuroscience appear to offer support to the kinds of mental descriptions offered by Polanyi. Koch points to our ability to capture peripheral visual input despite the sharp spotlight of attention aiming to some other, small portion of the visual field. Although talking specifically about vision, the same mechanism may apply to abstract mental states.

Does this same capacity explain the peripheral awareness of input identified by Polanyi as *subsidiary awareness*? I suspect this is the case. For now, we must remain satisfied with identifying subsidiary awareness as coming from the action of zombie agents. These subroutines in the brain are trained (through repetition) by starting with conscious recognition of particulars within working memory, then over time rendering them into a subsidiary form, and then finally *integrating* them together with other agents; the tacit integration! This action describes the gaining of comprehension. **When enough neurons fire in a linked collection of networks, consciousness is the result and we recognize that an understanding has taken place.** I have described a hypothesis here, not some final research conclusion, but the direction this kind of research is taking us is promising. The firing of many linked neural networks is included as part of the theory of *global neuronal workspace* (Dehaene, 2014). **The theory identifies the experience of consciousness as arising from the cascade of messaging between enormous numbers of neurons.** That gushing torrent occurs when all the different neuronal networks involved in a thought or perception suddenly agree among themselves. That coherence of agreement sets up intense communication between all these zombie agents leading to consciousness of the thought content.

The global neuronal workspace theory sent a gush of excitement through me as I recognized it as the key I am looking for to nail down the mystery of subsidiary particulars and their eventual tacit integration. During incubation, the various disconnected subsidiary particulars swarm around as a jumble of zombie agents. Suppose they all unconsciously discover a way for each other to fit together. Polanyi calls it the moment of tacit integration. The zombie agents now signal each other in a torrential cascade of electrical signals that force the discovery into consciousness. At that moment, the Aha takes over and we have an insight into the problem we have been working so hard to understand. Dehaene is describing the underlying neural mechanism that explains how intuition works and how the unconscious delivers a mysterious understanding to the light of day. I caution that application of the global neuronal workspace theory in this manner is still a hypothesis and considerable research needs to be done in order to transition the hypothesis into established science however this approach sure sounds right to me!

A recent study offers brain imaging measurement data reinforcing the suggestion that, when first learning a skill, the prefrontal cortex exhibits the use of conscious attention for learning the correct response to visual stimuli. Over time, practice gradually automates the process so that a different region in the cerebellum takes over. Combining the words of Polanyi and Koch, the necessary subsidiary particulars merge into multiple unconscious zombie agents. (Balsters & Ramnani, 2011).

Recall that descriptions of the insight moment mentioned earlier in this book included distinctly pleasurable feelings. A feeling of elation occurs in association with a sudden certainty of the correctness of the newly comprehended entity. Neuroscience is beginning to recognize the mechanism for this effect. In his book *How We Decide,* Jonah Lehrer reports on research identifying the orbitofrontal cortex as a connector between the Amygdala (which yields feeling states) and the comprehension occurring in the frontal cortex (Lehrer, 2009). When comprehension hits, the rational cortex is flooded with emotional content: Aha!

Due diligence is necessary when attempting to draw conclusions from neuroscience research; I have not found any evidence refuting the claims made by Polanyi. The most relevant discovery points to the large amount of unconscious mental processing happening among large collections of trained neurons, the zombie agents. These automated processes appear to offer a neuronal basis for the formation of tacit integrations.

Brain Lateralization or Right Brain/Left Brain

During the early sixties research by Sperry, Gazzaniga, and colleagues on the mental effects of splitting the brain in half through the corpus callosum gave rise to the split brain phase of cognitive interpretation; consequently, the right and left hemispheres were seen as offering some degree of specialization in behavior. The term "right brain vs. left brain" developed a common reference especially in the popular press. Allen Beaton in a review of laterality research (1985) describes a number of claimed descriptive dichotomies between the left and right hemispheres such as verbal versus non-verbal, linguistic versus spatial, serial versus parallel, analytic versus holistic, focal versus diffuse, and rational versus intuitive. These are certainly suggestive of the focal versus subsidiary awareness dichotomies that we have seen within the theory of tacit knowledge. Gill concluded that explicit knowing is a function of the left hemisphere of the brain; tacit knowing identified as a function of the right hemisphere (Gill, 1980). However much we may like this easy identity between brain lateralization and Polanyi's ideas, Beaton summarized a number of conflicting research results that argue against the simple identification of split-brain function with psychological processes. (Beaton, 1985). The brain hemispheres are after all quite thoroughly connected.

Despite this cautionary perspective, some evidence exists relating brain lateralization to the structure of tacit knowledge. Howard Gardner summarizes research with patients who have suffered right hemisphere strokes. He suggests that:

> They are unable to figure out the underlying architecture or composition, the nature of, and relationship between, the various parts and characters of a story. Instead, each part stands alone, a single brick unrelated to any other-or to the entire edifice. The difficulties patients have in relating different portions of the story to one another and integrating them into a coherent whole may well depend upon spatial mechanisms that are the province of the right brain (Gardner, 1981).

This description aligns with the idea of the right hemisphere offering the integrative function needed for the assembling of subsidiary particulars into a tacit whole. Subsidiary particulars are somehow tracked in the brain all at the same time - a form of **parallel processing** as opposed to the **linear processing** of focal awareness. Perhaps the zombie agents hypothesized to do this are somehow connected through right brain parallel processing. Considering the confusing and sometimes conflicting research into brain lateralization, we should be cautious in our application of these studies to the understanding of the structure of tacit knowledge. The zombie agents do not inhabit only one hemisphere vs. the other. Exercise considerable caution about attending to the "right brain – left brain" story.

Another research effort identified localized regions of the brain that fire when confronted with the "Aha!" insight moment that we associate with tacit integration. A measureable difference between the functioning of the right and left hemispheres suggests the right is offering subsidiary awareness of possible solutions to insight problems while the left hemisphere tends to overrun these possibilities with conscious but sometimes extraneous babble (Bowden E. M., Jung-Beeman, Fleck, & Kounios, 2005). This development derived from elaborately measured EEG and Functional Magnetic Resonance Imaging techniques applied to experimental subjects. They were asked to solve insight type problems and self-report if the solution popped into consciousness or occurred through conscious, analytical thought. The authors of the research summarized their results saying:

> In sum, when people solve problems with insight, leading to an "Aha" experience, their solutions are accompanied by a striking increase in neural activity in RH aSTG [*Right Hemisphere anterior superior temporal gyrus*]. Thus, within the network of cortical areas required for problem solving,

different components are engaged or emphasized when solving with, versus without, insight. We propose that the RH aSTG facilitates integration of information across distant lexical or semantic relations, allowing solvers to see connections that had previously eluded them. In the two millennia since Archimedes shouted "Eureka!", it has seemed common knowledge that people sometimes solve problems-whether great scientific questions or trivial puzzles-by a seemingly distinct mechanism called insight. This mechanism involves suddenly seeing a problem in a new light, often without awareness of how that new light was switched on. We have demonstrated that insight solutions are indeed associated with a discrete, distinct pattern of neural activity, supporting unique cognitive processes (Jung-Beeman, et al., 2004).

These studies into neuroscience are quite encouraging and suggest Polanyi's tacit integration has a recognizable neurological home. However, many scientists are critical of claims for the existence of mystical mumbo-jumbo causes for insight, including references to tacit knowledge. As we dig into academic research, attention must be paid to the skeptics as they challenge us to be sure about what we claim to be true.

The Critics Speak

Just as the tennis players best friend is a skilled opponent, we need to check to see if the research literature counters the ideas behind tacit knowledge with concerns and constructive criticism.

Perhaps a perceptual blindness has trapped us in a wish state regarding tacit knowledge and a critical review of the anti-tacit knowledge literature can straighten us out.

Critics of Polanyi have identified tacit knowledge as a subtle way to cloak the development of expertise and comprehension with fuzzy, mystical, internal mental events, hence defying sensible, scientific explanation. They claim the 'black box' of tacit knowledge and its cousin, intuition, offers little help to the student or teacher in the development of expertise. If colleagues are unable to verbalize expert actions, it is because they lack the appropriate tools to uncover what it is that they are doing, and/or the vocabulary needed to articulate it.

Taking this complaint to an extreme, Bruce Laduke denies that tacit knowledge is anything other than a choice, made by the possessor of that knowledge, to remain silent. He insists that claims describing tacit knowledge as something inexpressible is like knowledge existing within the realm of asking a question. This reductionist view fails to explain examples of expertise. Connoisseurs of fine art, when studying the puzzle of the supposedly ancient Greek statue that just "didn't look right," expressed an intuitive sense that the statue was not authentic (Gladwell, 2005). The various experts called in to examine the statue were not able to offer an explicit explanation for their unease. The negative judgments lay hidden within the tacit dimension. Considerable effort gradually uncovered the underlying issues (subsidiary particulars) leading to the negative assessment. At no time did any of these connoisseurs choose to remain silent about the cause of their suspicions; rather the judgments gradually seeped out of a subconscious state. Defining away tacit knowledge as the result of a decision not to communicate is inconsistent with too many published descriptions of tacit knowledge. We need not worry about this criticism.

Can Tacit Knowledge be converted into the explicit? A special field called "knowledge elicitation" (Hoffman & Lintern, 2006) use various tools for building a systematic representation of expert knowledge. One such tool, for example, is the concept map we have already encountered with Archimedes principle. Some knowledge elicitators scorn tacit knowledge as foolishness arising from metaphysical arguments found embedded in tangled philosophical weeds. Hoffman and Lintern go on to claim that inexpressible knowledge has never been demonstrated (I find that statement unconvincing). They recommend that tools such as concept mapping can support knowledge professionals in identifying and describing expert practice with adequate clarity. Extracting tacit knowledge requires conducting careful interviews with experts where the details of expert practice are teased out and made explicit.

My reply to these scoffers of tacit knowledge falls into two categories. First, recall the example of the cabinet makers in South Africa where the distinct sound made by a cutting tool on wood served as an indicator to the master craftsman how well the apprentice was doing. Can the knowledge elicitators capture that sound and the experienced judgment behind the sound in one of their concept-mapped boxes? I doubt it. Similarly, can a concept map pass along to someone from a distant planet what coffee smells like? Many other examples of direct experience are clearly untellable. Even a series of concept maps cannot capture the hidden knowledge of a chess master.

My second reaction is accommodative rather than dismissive. Active research groups in the field of corporate knowledge management offer a considerable body of published studies. These analyses include both the merits and negative impressions dismissing tacit knowledge. The arguments for and against tacit knowledge contain an interesting and useful component. Can you take the elusive tacit integration representing your comprehension of some complex entity and work it backwards untying the subsidiary particulars, looking at them under a mental microscope, and thus, ultimately reducing the "thing you cannot tell" into something that you *can* tell? Is the tacit convertible into the explicit? Hoffman & Lintern claim to be doing exactly that. Once you have experienced the "Aha!" moment and felt the tacit integration, you are then in a position to try to explain it to someone else. During such a process of explanation, you may discover that you know things that you *can* tell, things that you *can* put into words or write down on paper (as I am doing now), thus building an explanation of something you finally comprehend. I certainly can accommodate this argument

Making the tacit explicit is all very well - except that you run into the problem we had at the beginning of the book where you, as learner, tried to understand something but initially failed to understand it despite the efforts of the teacher and the book. After eventually achieving the tacit integration, you cannot turn around and force a new learner to jump across that same logical gap needed for constructing the tacit integration. It might seem to *you* that you know something you *can* tell, but the listener does not share that feeling because your explanation is not working for them. We end up full circle. You may indeed be able to work backwards untangling the subsidiary particulars and reconstructing them into a detailed and coherent explanation, but the new learners are still stuck needing to grab all those particulars required to build the internal tacit integration necessary for comprehension.

The arcane skill of chick sexing offers an example. David Eagleman mentioned this curiosity in his book *Incognito* (Eagleman, 2011) in which he described the great difficulty in quickly separating male chicks from the females) who are the valuable egg layers). Experts who claim not to know how they do it must separate thousands of chicks within about a half second each. The case of the inexplicable sexing procedure captured the attention of expert system analysts who ran some experiments on how the process is done. To be economically useful the sexers need to be 99% accurate. Training consisted of trial and error exposure to chicks with an expert simply agreeing or disagreeing with the trainee's choices. After several months of this exhausting repetition, the new sexers achieved 95% accuracy. Reaching the 99% level took an additional 2 to 6 years! In studying this case Biederman and Shiffrar (Biederman & Margaret, 1987) discovered that adding photographs to the instructional process, did offer significant help to the learners. Indeed, a group of completely untrained and uninvolved participants approached 84% accuracy by using these small sets of pictures rather quickly. In this manner, some of the so-called tacit knowledge was successfully placed into an explicit form. Reaching the 99% level of accuracy, however, requires learning how to judge extremely rare and weird examples. The critics make a point that you can speed up a tacit learning process through the addition of carefully constructed teaching aids. I agree that any content offerings helping to bring individual particulars into the mind, and that also alter perceptions into a subsidiary form, should aid the formation of tacit integrations.

Discussions about tacit knowledge may degenerate into playing a name game. Is a particular set of knowledge explicit or tacit? Perhaps Polanyi was more concerned about the structure of tacit knowledge as a *process* for cognitive behavior rather than as a categorization system. Stephen Gourlay offers valuable clarification on this point in a paper written to analyze a well-known knowledge management theory. He describes tacit knowledge more as a process than as a categorization of knowledge into one type or another (Gourlay, 2002).

Practice as process

Criticisms coming from educational and cognitive psychologists need careful attention. Return to the essence of learning keeping in mind the need to form a tacit integration of subsidiary particulars. One way to visualize tacit knowing as a process is to note the practice needed to bring it about. The process of practicing a musical instrument or practicing a ballet step is observable by anyone in the outside world. How do you see the practice when that effort is buried unseen inside the mind? Gourlay reminds us that practice is integral to tacit knowledge and he suggests that consuming and manipulating knowledge representations is a form of practicing. So when trying to gain that critical moment of insight, you "practice" the subsidiary particulars by reviewing them, juggling them, assessing them, indwelling in them, and hope unconscious zombie agents develop to work on them during incubation. This set of internal behaviors exhibit a form of practice not visible to the external world. The outcome of all this "practice" is the moment of tacit integration, the moment of insight.

New curricular methodologies aim at reducing the assignment of practice (called disparagingly "drill and kill"). Repetitive exercises are characterized today as boring, stultifying, and leading to a deadening of educational efforts. If carried too far, these attitudes dangerously short-circuit the need for practice when embedding particulars into the mind as well as getting them into a subsidiary form. Repetition (practice) is an essential component to learning.

An associated trap in educational design is the bugaboo of memorization (sometimes called learning by rote). I have always abhorred memorization. I recall the hateful task of memorizing the names of all the state capitals. How much better it would seem to me to ask for the *story* explaining how a particular city became the capital of a state. Our minds work well with stories and we remember stories far better than dry facts. A collection of stories about the creation of state capitals offers a strong likelihood for remembering their names in a meaningful manner. Joseph Novak created a course at Cornell University called; *Learning to Learn*, where he tried to move students away from doing what he disparagingly said was "rote memorization" (Wandersee & Novak, 2005) p.21. There may well be times when memorizing is necessary as in learning symbols for the chemical elements (Fe is iron, Ca is calcium etc.). If you do not know these in a hurry, you are unable to solve the balancing of chemical equations. If you must acquire many explicit facts, memorization is a way to get these particulars into the brain quickly. Once there, the hope is they eventually become subsidiary in nature and aid in forming tacit integrations. So once again individual students will have certain preferences in how they learn. The danger is that learning might stop at memorization and *meaningful* learning is then stifled.

Earlier in the book when discussing constructivism, I described the educational practice of inquiry learning as an example of the application of tacit knowledge. Some educational theorists attack inquiry as an inefficient learning approach and, hence, seem to be attacking tacit knowledge although not by name. Read the title of a research study published in the journal *Educational Psychologist*. It challenges us with "Why Minimal Guidance during Instruction Does Not Work: An Analysis of the Failure of Constructivist, Discovery, Problem-Based, Experiential, and Inquiry-Based Teaching" (Kirschner, Sweller, & Clark, 2006). Whew! That's a heavy claim dumped on us in the midst of our constructivist-laden views regarding the importance of tacit knowledge. How do we save the day?

At least the authors agree that constructivism accurately describes the process of learning but then complain that too many instructional strategies turn learners loose on the environment with essentially no guidance. They offer a number of research studies showing the superior educational attainment of students undergoing **direct instruction** instead of **discovery** type teaching. Direct instruction means a process of explicitly showing students what to do, how to do it, and what to know. Some ways of accomplishing these tasks include offering worked out examples of problems and using worksheets (are we back again to cookbook lab exercises?). The movement away from discovery learning is partially energized by the well-known characteristic of the brain, a small short-term memory, along with the claim that learning is just transferring stuff into long-term memory. Simple, just tell them what they need to know and then give a test on it!

If I begin to sound petulant, I am being unfair to the critical article since they have a point, but the criticism is muddled by a vague categorization of what we mean by discovery. A reply to this study, (Hmelo-Silver, Duncan, & Chinn, 2007), identifies two sources of confusion. Too many otherwise distinct pedagogical strategies were all lumped together into one nasty category of extreme discovery mode in which students are dumped into an ocean of undigested information to sink or swim unattended. Pure discovery does have this characteristic and is measurably inefficient. However, learning through *guided* inquiry allows for a great deal of instructor involvement at each step as the students grope toward understanding. The various aids on this journey are called "scaffolding" in the educational literature. The rungs of the scaffold include necessary behaviors of coaching and other parts of the relationship between master and apprentice. The other flaw in the study suggests a selectivity effect where the authors left out some research studies that found guided (scaffolded) inquiry to be demonstrating greater measurable effectiveness than direct instruction. Therefore, constructivism is apparently not always bad; it depends on how extreme you take the philosophy.

In another article (Mayer, 2004), an additional complaint is lodged against constructivism, not for its view of learning but for discouraging modalities of learning other than pure inquiry. Mayer helpfully clarifies that constructivism does not inherently force requirements on (or limit the methodology for) how learners gain the necessary information to construct knowledge. I remind the reader that near the beginning of this book I said all modalities of information transfer are fair game for gathering the subsidiary particulars needed to form the tacit integration. In some cases, depending on the prior understandings of the learner, direct instruction via lecture or readings from a book can offer the appropriate form and content needed to add critical subsidiary particulars to the repertoire of a student. I warned against a tendency for educator theorists to insist that a certain mode of instruction is the only true, right, and sanctioned way to bring about understanding. The existence of instructional regulations limiting behavior serves to flag that sanctioned instructional technique as a fad. As a philosophy of learning, constructivism is consistent with the tacit theory of knowledge. There are no artificial barriers to types and techniques of learning. It all depends on what the mind of the learner contains. Hopefully all the subsidiary particulars needed for creating a tacit integration are in there. Some students will need direct hands-on exposure to the content or others may need to organize for themselves some of these particulars while yet others need someone to simply show them the way. In the end, tacit integration is what that leads to insight and whatever it takes to get there is proper.

So the critics of constructivism rightfully complain when adherents place constraints and straightjackets onto those who embrace it. Complaints are currently directed against educators over this issue expressing the concern that teacher training curricula push discovery over the business of hard work memorizing the times tables. If everyone understood the tacit nature of learning, this false dichotomy of how to do it should dissipate.

I have searched for evidence that Michael Polanyi's description of tacit knowledge is somehow out of date, incorrect, of no value, or destroyed by the latest discoveries in psychology, neurology, philosophy, and all other 'ologies out there and am now satisfied that Polanyi is as right today as he was in 1958!

Begin Here →

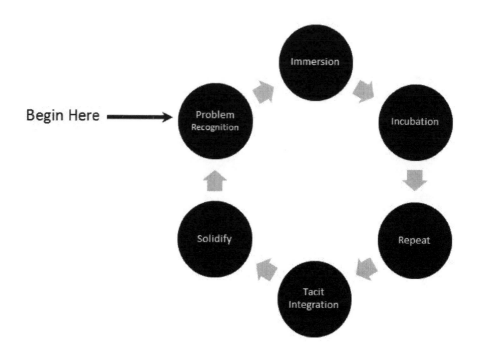

Cycle of Comprehension

Chapter Six: Controversies

In a 1789 letter to Jean-Baptise Leroy, Benjamin Franklin gave birth to the famous saying "but in this world nothing can be said to be certain, except death and taxes." Today I feel safe in adding a third element to that small list which is the ubiquitous expression of dissatisfaction over the current state of education. You can find the complaints everywhere and in every decade. CNN screamed a headline, "What's Wrong with America's Schools?" You can watch a 20/20 video expose on UTUBE with the catchy title, "Stupid in America; What's Wrong with the U.S. Education System?" The John William Pope Center warns that a recent study concludes that American education schools are an industry of mediocrity. How can this dissatisfaction continue cranking away after decades upon decades of research on how to teach, decades upon decades of experimentation on teaching and learning and the expenditure of hundreds of billions of dollars?

No matter how the pendulum swings, Tacit Knowledge can help

We have examined the features of the tacit theory of knowledge and while on that journey have used this theory as a lens to sort through the pedagogy typical of what we might call standard instruction vs anything different or new.

Bruce Torff characterized essentially all pedagogies into two broad categories: "externalist" and "intersubjectivist" (Torff, 1999). The externalist perspective views the knowledge to be gained by the learner as preexisting and outside the learner. The job of the instructional system is to transfer the knowledge from the outside and get it inside the learners head; therefore, the role of the teacher and textbook is paramount. To put this into a historical perspective look back to the schooling in the late nineteenth century where one room school houses catered to students who were lectured to and had to recite their memorized lessons by rote. On the other hand, the intersubjectivist position shines a spotlight first on what goes on inside the head of the learner where the knowledge "out there" is constructed "in here", inside the brain with considerable help from other learners in a collaboration of comprehension development.

Historically, in the early twentieth century, John Dewey introduced key ideas of *progressivism* and shifted attention away from the teacher to the student. That pendulum swings back and forth in various guises from decade to decade. Today the practitioners of an externalist perspective are convinced that "direct instruction" is the correct way to go. Teachers explain, lecture, supervise, and give practice exercises and homework. The contemporary "constructivist" follows in the footsteps of Dewey, much to the consternation of the more conservative adherents of direct instruction. Formal educational research bats the ball back and forth, depending on how the teaching experiments are designed and analyzed.

Since I have already identified constructivism as following logically from the tacit theory of knowledge, you may expect that I will be sympathetic to constructivist pedagogy but not without some considerable qualifications. At the outset I must set aside judgments regarding selection of the material to be covered. For example, as I write this book, the new "Common Core" curriculum is much in the news and is raising controversy. Some of that dissension is about the choice of content to be taught in the schools. Tacit knowledge will not help us with that part of the problem.

What does tacit knowledge suggest we do when it comes to designing the "how" of teaching while leaving out the "what?"

Unexploded bombs litter the path we must carefully tread in the effort to untangle the *how* knot. Intersubjectivists use technical phrases that sound terrible to those preferring direct instruction. How about a constructivist claim that knowledge is "socially constructed," "created collaboratively," and "negotiated with others?" Does this mean that 2+2 is negotiated to equal four? Or, even worse, could 2+2 be collaboratively constructed to equal five? A quick answer to this challenge of apparent nonsense is certainly no.

The tacit theory of knowledge calls upon us to remember the need to form a tacit integration, hence, possibly generating an "Aha" moment. This goal is aided by working with others in a collaborative sense. Small groups of learners talking among themselves help each other clarify the subsidiary particulars and, thus, assist in the formation of comprehension. The collaboration offers feedback on missing particulars and misconceptions that block integration. One critical member of the collaborative team is the teacher who slips from one small group to another listening and coaching. This practice is not as scary as the term "socially constructed" initially suggests. A subset of educators whom we may call "radical constructivists" may even deny the idea that facts exist outside of our brains, but that extreme view is one I am comfortable to safely set aside. My suggestion is to be careful before throwing out too quickly what sounds like mushy lunacy because its meaning might not be what it sounds like.

Going back to the externalists who promote **direct instruction**, we find a clear directive to have strong teacher leaders offering carefully crafted lessons that show learners exactly what they need to know and understand. Research on this approach (recognized as similar to the way we were taught back in the olden days) offers data apparently showing its superiority over the socially constructed voodoo of mushy progressivity so popular in schools of education today. What can possibly be wrong about such a time tested approach? It all depends on how the method is handled by a teacher. Direct instruction carries the danger of developing rote learning behaviors without building associated comprehension. Direct instruction can be reassuring to teachers who have a specific and clear outline of what to do and how to do it. On the other hand zealous administrators can force teachers into a rigid, rule-based system of behavior better followed by a robot.

While a detailed analysis of varied curricular offerings, an overwhelming task, would be a useful tool, it is way beyond the scope of this book. Let us agree that the ultimate aim for learners is to acquire comprehension and the capacity to think, communicate, and work with others, regardless of the competing methodologies. Since comprehension is the goal, as long as tacit integrations are taking place you know you are on the right track.

At the End

Tacit knowledge is a means to another end. A test for the presence or activation of tacit knowledge is found in *Flow*. The key discoverer and proponent of this idea is the psychologist Mihaly Csikszentmihalyi (chick-SENT-me-high) whose work you want to become familiar with if you have not already done so (Csikszentmihalyi, 1997). He elucidates the mental state of being "in the zone." When in this state, a person is intently involved in tasks that are so engrossing that time melts away, the surroundings are no longer intrusive, and the actions undertaken seem effortless yet require extreme concentration. I claim that tacit knowledge is operating under these circumstances and, hence, leads to experiences later described by the active participant as highly pleasurable. Csikszentmihalyi describes this flow experience as a magnet for learning and offers additional clues to what we may wish to put into place for encouraging tacit integrations. As usual, he does not reference the tacit theory of knowledge.

To get into flow the participant confronts a series of systematic tasks leading to a desired end, for example mastering a skill in the arts, athletics, or abstract problem solving. As these tasks are accomplished, immediate feedback indicates success or the need for response adjustment. Flow occurs if skills happen to be closely matched to the demands of the task so that the participant is neither bored nor overwhelmed with failure. For example, consider the rock climber who faces a new cliff presenting difficulties but not beyond the capability of the climber. If the climb is too easy the mind wanders but if too difficult, frustration sets in (perhaps dangerously so). Similarly, the application of a newly acquired tacit integration in any area of human endeavor (illustrated below) strengthens the learning while reinforcing the delight in making the leap across a conceptual gap. The appeal of computer-based games comes from the immediate feedback as well as the need for skill in aiming guns at the enemy; hence the participant gets into the flow state, which is highly satisfying.

I will illustrate this linkage between tacit knowledge and flow with a story from my own experience. One of my lifelong hobby interests is found within Community Theater. Some of my most memorable and rewarding moments occurred at Oglebay Institute's Towngate Theater in Wheeling, West Virginia. Under the inspired direction of Harold O'Leary, the Towngate produced some exceptionally fine performances of classic plays such as Eugene O'Neal's *Long Day's Journey into Night*. My specialty there was lighting design, and I sat in the light booth night after night watching the performance and twiddling the knobs on variable transformers to change light levels as the play progressed. During rehearsals a carefully prepared cue sheet indicated which knobs were to be rotated and to which level, depending on specific events taking place on stage. Working through these cues in rehearsal was a focused effort sometimes resulting in corrections to errors or revisions to the lighting design. Eventually repeated practice automated my mind to the changes in light levels so that each knob gained a status as a subsidiary particular. When working with the elements of the performance onstage, I was able to get into a flow state during performances and adjusted light levels without reference to the cue sheets anymore. In effect, I became a performer alongside actors on the stage. The controlling of light levels was subsidiary to the mood on the stage, which became the aim of my focal attention. I employed Polanyi's sense of indwelling in the production and adjusted lighting to fit the particular performance occurring that night. Some actors later took note of the subtle variations in lighting taking place and commented favorably on the degree of involvement I was exhibiting. I know what it means to be "in the zone," as Csikszentmihalyi put it, relying upon tacit awareness of the subsidiary particulars as Polanyi would put it. These concepts work together and the resulting desired flow state is an unforgettable special experience.

The task of learning something new leading up to the achievement of a tacit integration is best accomplished under the flow state during which the learner is serious and engaged. Maximizing flow in one's life can lead toward greater happiness. The state of being in flow is self-motivating and, hence, is a desired state for the best kind of learning to take place. Csikszentmihalyi measured flow states for many subjects and found the most common condition for that state to occur was either at work (who would have thought?) or when a hobby was actively pursued. Learning and teaching can be exceptionally rewarding when searching intently for tacit integrations. Keep looking for the "Aha" experience in your life!

My search for modern confirmation of the wisdom shown by Polanyi in his introspections is over but never complete. Just as these last paragraphs finished, I stumbled across a fantastic book by Barbara Oakley who is an engineering professor. I metaphorically climbed a mountain using Polanyi as guide only to find someone else at the top who climbed up the other side. Oakley relies directly on the research in cognitive psychology and neuroscience and came to the same place. She describes the view using different words but what we are seeing is essentially the same. Her book is easier for a student to understand since Polanyi uses some terminology (like subsidiary particulars) that is harder to follow so I must commend her book most highly. It is called: *A Mind for Numbers How to Excel at Math and Science* published by Penguin in 2014. There is an online course offering some of this material which is also highly recommended: **https://class.coursera.org/learning-001/lecture/99**

Suggested Readings:

PERSONAL KNOWLEDGE

This is Polanyi's "magnum opus," a scholarly compendium on his views regarding tacit knowledge embedded within his encompassing philosophy of science. His objective was to add an element of "personal knowledge" into the way we view science thus taking away from science the sense of impersonal objectivity with which the field is normally perceived. This book is not the best place to begin exploring Polanyi's thought unless you prefer a scholarly type of writing. He discusses intellectual passions, beliefs, and applications of his philosophy to politics and religion as well as art. A critic complained his ideas are not well organized here nor fully supported but I find fascinating nuggets of insight throughout. The depth of his analysis makes this my desert island book. I can read and reread it over and over again continually finding new inspiration from the fascinating content. The book is published by the University of Chicago Press with an updated printing in 1962.

THE TACIT DIMENSION

We have here a slender little volume offering in the first forty pages or so an accessible description of tacit knowledge from the pen of the master. The last fifty pages explore the subject from a philosophical standpoint. Polanyi discusses evolution and the problem of a creative mind recognizing dim possibilities for a coherence not yet understood yet there to be believed. In this manner he develops a perspective on the philosophy of science. The book was based on a series of lectures prepared for Yale University and was printed in 1967 by Anchor Books (Doubleday and Company).

MEANING

Polanyi joined up with Harry Prosch in the last explication of his thinking where he pulls from earlier writings and extends them. The unifying core of this book concerns intellectual freedom. The structure of tacit knowledge is applied to art, myth, religion and authority. This work is based upon lectures given at the University of Texas and Chicago. The book is rather advanced and demands considerable cognitive care on the part of the reader. Polanyi shows how the ideals of science (as exemplified by a devotion to objectivity) are misleading when viewed through the lens of personal knowledge. Herein is found one of the more complete explanations of tacit knowing. This is another University of Chicago Press publication printed in 1975.

TACIT KNOWING: IT'S BEARING ON SOME PROBLEMS OF PHILOSOPHY

Curiously this article is one of his easiest to understand yet was published in a scientific journal called *Reviews of Modern Physics* (Vol. 1, Number 4, Oct 1962, pages 601 -616). He covers the whole explanation of tacit knowledge in a friendly manner and points to applications in the philosophy of science and engineering. This essay is also found in a valuable set of collected works of

Polanyi called *Knowing and Being* edited by Marjorie Grene and published in 1969 by the University of Chicago Press.

MICHAEL POLANYI SCIENTIST AND PHILOSOPHER

This book is the complete biography of the life of Polanyi embedded within a comprehensive review of his intellectual pursuits. William T. Scott is the primary author and as a physicist he brings the capacity to write in detail about the scientific side of the research Polanyi performed as a physical chemist. Martin X. Moleski took over the task of completing the biography, which had grown to nearly 300,000 words. Some readers will be bogged down in the scientific side of the book, which is quite comprehensive. Moleski pared down the massive manuscript to a manageable size and offers to the project his personal background in theology and philosophy. The book begins with great grandparents and weaves a fascinating story of the family working forward in time. Sometimes so many people (aunts, uncles, and siblings) show up that it can be hard to keep track of everyone. I think we get an effective picture of what led to the intellectual development of Polanyi. Many world-shaking events periodically shatter the lives of the family. We gain a perspective on why Polanyi felt the need to back away from physical chemistry and branch out into economics, social science, and philosophy. The book traces all aspects of the life of Polanyi right to the very end. I found the linkage between his invited talks and subsequent writings quite helpful in understanding his development as a philosopher. The book was published in 2005 by Oxford University Press.

MICHAEL POLANYI THE ART OF KNOWING

Understanding the thought of Michael Polanyi is quite challenging. Polanyi spares us a little because he did not grow up inside the academic worldview of the professional philosopher, yet his ideas are still often subtle and hard to grasp. Books such as this one help untangle the complexities and help guide a careful reader through his considerable output. Mark Mitchell weaves brief biographical summaries within an introduction to what Polanyi was thinking and how he came up with his ideas. The breadth and scope of his thought ranges over economics, politics, science, morality, religion, and of course the philosophy of knowledge and meaning. This book is part of the ongoing "Library of Modern Thinkers" series published by ISI Books IN 2006.

THE WAY OF DISCOVERY

This is another book introducing the thought of Polanyi with occasional forays into personal details of his life. Richard Gelwick is a professor of religion and philosophy and his book reflects that background with philosophical discussions on the thought of Polanyi. He includes reviews of other writings by either Polanyi or those who respond to implications of the theory of tacit knowledge. He attempts to judge where the teachings of Polanyi fit today. The emphasis is on religious, ethical, and social dimensions as seen through the eyes of an observer in 1977. The book was published by Oxford University Press.

IMPLICIT LEARNING AND TACIT KNOWLEDGE

Arthur Reber is a psychologist studying unconscious processes of the mind and is a specialist in tacit knowledge. This book is a scholarly review of psychological research in the field. It is part of the Oxford University Press series Vol. 19, 1993. Reber is concerned with implicit learning, which is a type of learning not reliant upon conscious processing. The term *implicit* can be viewed as modern psychological lingo for *tacit*. He introduces Polanyi and utilizes the structure of tacit knowledge in his research. Reber takes his place among a special group of research scientists exploring a subject recently forgotten hence offering little interest in psychology. The book is accessible despite being a professional review of the literature.

TACIT AND EXPLICIT KNOWLEDGE

Harry Collins is a current expert on tacit knowledge; his book is a major contribution to the field clarifying and establishing new ground. He examines very carefully the difference between tacit and explicit and is able to tease out three kinds of tacit knowledge. This work is an outcome of a study on the nature of expertise. It is not a particularly easy read but contains the latest thinking in the field and makes a considerable contribution to the analysis of tacit knowledge. Published by the University of Chicago Press, the 2010 date is an indicator of fresh interest in the field of tacit knowledge.

TACIT KNOWLEDGE IN ORGANIZATIONS

One of the rare areas of professional activity that openly references tacit knowledge is the field of information management within business applications. Companies have considerable trouble retaining valuable knowledge in an era of outsourcing and downsizing. Philippe Baumard is a professor of strategic management in France and offers four case studies in the recognition and protection of tacit knowledge within business settings. He is also concerned with expertise and writes a book that will appeal primarily to scholars of management theory. SAGE Publications offers an English translation reprinted in 2001.

TACIT KNOWLEDGE IN PROFESSIONAL PRACTICE

Robert Sternberg is a mountain of genius within the field of psychology and has a significant publishing record in tacit knowledge. Here he teams up with a practitioner at IBM, Joseph Horvath, and offers a series of articles by many experts in knowledge management and expertise. Tacit knowledge is analyzed within the context of professional endeavors across a wide spectrum including law, the military, medicine, management, sales, and teaching. I wish I had more time than what is likely offered to me over the remaining years of my life to dig into all the work published by Sternberg and others into their perspectives on tacit knowledge. This book is a significant rich source of additional insights to chew upon and was published in 1999 by Lawrence Erlbaum Associates.

ENABLING KNOWLEDGE CREATION

How to unlock the Mystery of Tacit Knowledge and Release the Power of Innovation is the subtitle of this ambitious study on extending the management of knowledge to the creation of new knowledge all within a perspective of the tacit side to knowledge. Another business oriented management study; this is not an easy read but offers many practical examples of tacit knowledge in corporate settings. Georg Von Krogh, Kazuo Ichijo, and Ikujiro Nonaka have globally recognized credentials in this field of study. The book is published by Oxford University Press in 2000.

I think you begin to see how little time we have to study all the published material on tacit knowledge and the listing here is the proverbial tip of a surprisingly huge iceberg. You are invited to plunge in!

I will work to update this information at my website at *www.tacitknowledge.org*

Works Cited

Anderson, L. W., Krathwohl, D. R., Airasian, P. W., Cruikshank, K. A., Meyer, R. E., Pintrich, P. R., . . . Wittrock, M. C. (Eds.). (2002). *A Taxonomy for Learning, Teaching, and Assessing: A revision of Bloom's Taxonomy of Educational Objectives, Complete Edition.* NY, New York: Longman.

Ash, K. I., & Wiley, J. (2006). The Nature of Restructuring in Insight: An Individual Differences Approach. *Psychonomic Bulletin & Review, 13*(1), 66-73.

Azad, K. (2013, August 12). *Understanding the Monty Hall Problem.* Retrieved from Better Explained Learn right not rote!: www.betterexplained.com/articles/understanding-the-monty-hall-problem/

Balsters, J. H., & Ramnani, N. (2011, February 9). Cerebellar Plasticity and the Automation of First-Order Rules. *The Journal of Neuroscience, 31*(6), pp. 2305-2312. Retrieved

September 4, 2012, from

http:/www.sciencedaily.com/releases/2011/02/1102090826

34.htm

Beardsley, M. C. (1975). *Thinking Straight Principles of Reasoning*

for Readers and Writers. Englewood Cliffs: Prentice-Hall.

Beaton, A. (1985). *Left Side Right Side A Review of Laterality*

Research. New Haven, Connecticut: Yale University Press.

Biederman, I., & Margaret, M. S. (1987). Sexing Day-Old Chicks: A

Case Study and Expert Systems Analysis of a Difficult

Perceptual Learning Task. *Journal of Experimental*

Psychology, Learning, memory,and Cognition, 13(4), 640-

645.

Bloom, S. (Ed.). (1954). *Taxonomy of Educational Objectives*

Cognitive Domain (Vol. 1). New York: Longman Inc.

Bowden, E. M., Jung-Beeman, M., Fleck, J., & Kounios, J. (2005, July). New approaches to Demystifying Insight. *Trends in Cognitive Sciences, 9*(7), 322-328.

Bowden, M. E., Jung-Beeman, M., Fleck, J., & Kounios, J. (2005). New Approaches to Demystifying Insight. *Trends in Cognitive Science, 9*(7), 322-328.

Bullock, S. (1905, July/September). The Development of Steam Navigation. *The Connecticut Magazine, IX*(3), pp. 440-455.

Buonomano, D. (2012). *Brain Bugs How the Brain's Flaws Shape Our Lives.* NewYork, NY: W. W. Norton & Co, Norton Paperback.

Burbules, N. (2008). Tacit Teaching. *Educational Philosophy and Theory, 40*(5), 666-677.

Busey, D. (2013, July 9). Retrieved from http://lumberjocks.com/hopdevil/projects

Csikszentmihalyi, M. (1997). *Finding Flow.* New York, NY: Basic Books, Perseus Books Group.

Dehaene, S. (2014). *Consciousness and the Brain deciphering How the Brain Codes Our Thoughts.* New York, NY: Viking Penguin.

Dreyfus, H. L., & Dreyfus, S. E. (1986). *Mind Over Machine The Power of Human Intuition and Expertise in the Era of the Computer.* New York: The Free Press.

Eagleman, D. (2011). *Incognito The secret Lives of the Brain.* New York, NY: Vintage Books.

eSystems, W. (2013, July 28). *iRespond Snap! Assessment.* Retrieved from Interactive learning: www.irespond.com

Faflick, P. (1982, October). Opening the "Trapdoor Knapsack". *Time,* p. 88.

Gamble, J. (2001). Modeling the Invisible: the pedagogy of craft apprenticeship. *Studies in Continuing Education, 23*(2), 185-200.

Gardner, H. (1981, February). How the Split Brain Gets a Joke. *Psychology Today*, pp. 74-78.

Gigerenzer, G. (2007). *Gut Feelings.* New York: Penguin Group.

Gill, J. H. (1980). Of Split Brains and Tacit Knowing. *International Philosophical Quarterly, 20*, 49-58.

Gladwell, M. (2005). *Blink.* NY, NY: Little, Brown and Company.

Gleick, J. (1992). *Genius The Life and Science of Richard Feynman.* New York: Pantheon Books.

Gourlay, S. (2002). Tacit Knowledge, Tacit Knowing or Behaving? *3rd European Organizational Knowledge, Learning Capabilities Conference*, (pp. 1-24). Athens, Greece.

Gurr, H. (2008, August 20). *Henry Gurr Professor of Physics.* Retrieved 2012, from University of South Carolina Aiken: http://www.usca.edu/math/~mathdept/hsg/

Hadamard, J. (1973). *The Mathematicians Mind. The Psychology of Invention in the Mathematical Field.* Princeton, NJ: Princeton University Press.

Halford, G. S., Baker, R., McCredden, J. E., & Bain, J. D. (2005, January). How Many Variables Can Humans Process? *Psychological Science, 16*(1), 70-76.

Harvey, S., & Goudvis, A. (2007). *Strategies That Work teaching Comprehension For Understanding and Engagement.* Portland, Maine: Stenhouse publishers.

Heath, T. L. (Ed.). (1897). *The Works of Archimedes Edited in Modern Notation With Introductory Chapters.* Cambridge, England: Cambridge University Press.

Hitt, J. (2012). *Bunch of Amateurs.* New York: Crown Publishers.

Hmelo-Silver, C. E., Duncan, R. G., & Chinn, C. A. (2007). Scaffolding and Achievement in Problem-Based and Inquiry Learning: A

Response to Kirschner, Sweller, and Clark (2006).

Educational Psychologist, 42(2), 99-107.

Hoffman, R. R., & Lintern, G. (2006). Eliciting and Representing the

Knowledge of Experts. In K. A. Ericsson, N. Charness, P.

Feltovich, & R. Hoffman (Eds.), *Cambridge Handbook of*

Expertise and Expert Performance (pp. 203-222). Cambridge

University Press.

Isaacson, W. (2008). *Einstein His Life and Universe.* New York: Simon

& Schuster.

Jenkins, L. (2005). *Permission to Forget.* Milwaukee: American

Society of Quality, Quality Press.

Jones, D. (2012). *The Aha! Moment A Scientists Take On Creativity.*

Baltimore, MD: The Johns Hopkins University Press.

Jung-Beeman, M., Bowden, E. M., Haberman, J., Frymiare, J. L.,

Arambel-Liu, S., Greenblatt, R., . . . Kounios, J. (2004). Neural

Activity When People Solve Verbal Problems with Insight.

Public Library of Science - Biology, 2(4), 500-510. Retrieved

from http://biology-plosjournals.org

Kawasaki, G., & Welch, S. (2013). *APE How to Publish a Book.*

Lexington, Ky: NONONINA PRESS. Retrieved from

http://epethebook.com

Kirschner, P. A., Sweller, J., & Clark, R. E. (2006). Why Minimal

Guidance During Instruction Does Not Work: An Analysis of

the Failure of Constructivist, Discovery, Problem-based,

Experiential, and Inquiry-Based Teaching. *Educational*

Psychologist, 41(2), 75-86.

Koch, C. (2012). *Consciousness Confessions of a Romantic*

Reductionist. Cambridge, MA: MIT Press.

Laduke, B. (2005, July/August). Beyond Polanyi. *Knowledge*

Management, 10,11.

Lehrer, J. (2009). *How We Decide.* New York, New York: Mariner

Books Houghton Mifflin Harcourt.

Loughlin, M. (2010). Epistemology, Biology and Mysticism: Comments on 'Polanyi's Tacit knowledge and the Relevance of Epistomology to Clinical Practice'. *Journal of Evaluation in Clinical Practice, 16*, 298-300.

Martin, D. J. (2012). *Elementary Science Methods A Constructivist Approach* (6 ed.). Belmont, CA: Wadsworth Cengage Learning.

Mayer, R. E. (2004, January). Should There Be a Three-Strikes Rule Against Pure Discovery Learning? *American Psychologist, 59*(1), 14-19.

Mednick, M. &. (1967). *Examiners Manual: Remote Associates Test.* Boston: Hought Mifflin.

Mlodinow, L. (2012). *Subliminal.* New York: Pantheon Books of Random House.

Perkins, D. (2000). *The Eureka Effect. The Art and Logic of Breakthrough Thinking.* New York: W. W. Norton & Company.

Pira, F. L. (2011). Entrepreneurial Intuition: An empirical Approach. *Journal of Management and Marketing Research, 6*, pp. 1-22.

Poincare, H. (1913). *The Foundations of Science.* New York: The Science Press.

Polanyi, J. C. (2005, Spring). Michael Polanyi, the Scientist. *Chemical Heritage, 23(1)*, 10-13. Philadelphia, PA.

Polanyi, M. (1962). *Personal Knowledge* (Corrected Edition ed.). Chicago: University of Chicago Press.

Polanyi, M. (1967). *The Tacit Dimension.* Garden City, New York: Anchor Books, Doubleday & Company.

Rawlinson, G. E. (1976). *The Significance of Letter Position in Word Recognition.* University of Nottingham. Nottingham, UK: Unpublished Doctoral Dissertation.

Scott, W. T. (1983). Michael Polanyi's Creativity in Chemistry. In R. Aris (Ed.), *Springs of Scientific Creativity* (pp. 279-307). Minneapolis, Minnesota: University of Minnesota Press.

Sio, U. N., & Ormerod, T. C. (2009). Does Incubation Enhance Problem Solving? A Meta-Analytic Review. *Psychological Bulletin, 125*(1), 94-120.

Smith, J. D., Zakrzewski, A. C., Roeder, J. L., Church, B. A., & Ashby, F. G. (2013). Deferred Feedback Sharply Dissociates Implicit and Explicit Category Learning. *Psychological Science, 25*(2), 447. doi:10.1177/0956797613509112

Specified, N. (n.d.). *The Monty Hall problem.* Retrieved September 21, 2012, from Wikipedia: Wilikedia.org/wiki/Monty_Hall_problem

Spickler, T. R. (1983, October 24). An Experiment on the Efficacy of Intuition Development in Improving Higher Levels of Learning and Reasoning in Physical Science. *Unpublished Doctoral Dissertation, West Virginia University*. Ann Arbor, Michigan, USA: University Microfilms International.

Stepzinski, T. (2006, Oct 30). *Florida Times Union*, p. B1.

Sternberg, R. J., & Davidson, J. E. (Eds.). (1995). *The Nature of Insight*. Cambridge, Mass: A Bradford Book, MIT Press.

Tobias, S. (1978). *Overcoming Math Anxiety*. Boston: Houghton Mifflin Company.

Topolinski, S., & Reber, R. (2010). Gaining Insight into the "Aha" Experience. *Current Directions in Psychological Science, 19*, 402-405.

Torff, B. (1999). Tacit Knowledge in Teaching: Folk Pedagogy and Teacher Education. In R. J. Sternberg, & J. A. Horvath, *Tacit*

Knowledge in Professional Practice (pp. 195-213). Mahwah,
New jersey: Lawrence Erlbaum Associates.

Waldrop, M. (1984). Before the Beginning. *Science, 5*, 45.

Wandersee, J. H., & Novak, J. J. (2005). *Teaching Science for
Understanding A Human Constructivist View.* (J. J. Mintzes,
Ed.) Burlington, MA: Elsever Academic Press.

Weisstein, E. W. (n.d.). *Young Girl- Old Woman Illusion.* Retrieved
June 21, 2013, from MathWorld - A Wolfram web Resource:
http://mathworld_Wolfram.com/YoungGirl-
OldWomenIllusion.html

INDEX

Made in the USA
Lexington, KY
03 November 2015